Choose to Lead

A Guide to Awakening the Leader Within

Kathleen Schafer

Choose to Lead:

A 28-Day Guide to Awakening the Leader Within

Copywrite© 2015 by Kathleen Schafer

The views expressed in this book are the author's and are intended for educational purposes only.

First Printing: November 2015

ISBN:978-1518722127

This book is dedicated to the beautiful, bold, brilliant women in my life who have stuck by me as I have chosen to lead. They inspire me to continue living my life of service with joy. Through the sharing of their leadership with me, we have enriched the lives of many and for that, I am forever grateful.

Acknowledgments

As I progress through my life and expand my leadership, I constantly reminded of the importance of those in my life who contribute so much to the person I am. A few words of gratitude only scratch the surface of the immense love and appreciation I have for those who have helped create this book and the good it will bring to those who read it and beyond.

- Marla Wald, who continues to stand beside me through life with words of support, encouragement and strength
- Traci David, who brings a presence, strength and compassion that allows me to own my leadership
- Sabrina DeLay, who has embraced these practices in her own life and has contributed enormously by supporting me to bring the lessons of this book forward with greater clarity
- Lisa Arfaa, whose vision allowed me to see the call for this work with the young and continues to inspire their learning of it to create leaders for generations to come
- Susan Henkels, whose friendship and collaboration gave birth to the "what if nothing is wrong with you concept"
- Aaron Paquette for taking the time to edit the book and let me know its value from the outset
- Paul McKay and the Integrated Web Strategy team that are bringing the book to life with creativity, insight and professionalism
- To my clients, students, and audiences around the world, I am inspired by your optimism, your strength and your belief that the world can be better—that we can be better. It is your call that my work answers and will continue to do so.

Thoughts to Start You on the Journey

The most important journey for you to make in your life is the one that takes you inside of yourself—to know and understand the person you are and how to be at your best every day. The key to leading in your life is making the choice to be your best first and then allowing what you want to create to manifest, as you desire. It is not the other way around; without inner clarity, no amount of external success will quell the ache of feeling that there is something more.

It is not necessary to hit rock bottom before you learn to see your light and confidently put it into the world. Although in the past, it may have been the only way for you to let yourself see your life in a different way. How beautiful would it be if you allowed yourself the opportunity to explore your gifts, talents and innate strengths, without the agony of struggling to achieve outside validation and the resulting failure to be happy? This book is about that opportunity to make these discoveries now and to begin leading in your life. If there were not some part of you with which you were dissatisfied, you would not have picked up this book. Some part of you knew that something needed to be unearthed, to be shifted in a way that allowed you to discover some bright, shining piece that has been hidden away, a part that is longing to be of service in the world.

How do you begin the journey? The first step is knowing that every day is a new opportunity, a new chance to be in the creative process of living, loving and giving in the best possible way; in other words, to lead. You must understand that at no point will you ever "arrive" at the end. There is no goal that can be obtained that stops this process, because only death in this life ends the physical cycle of growth, change and evolution. So if you truly understand that there is no end point, there is nothing that can be achieved that makes you a winner and ends the game, then you can relax, as each day becomes an exciting gift in the creative process; each day becomes an opportunity to build upon your desires and dreams.

Congratulations on taking the first step toward acknowledging this truth. The journey on which you are embarking will be as challenging and overwhelming as you make it—and it is your journey. You must decide if you wish to proceed through all 28 days in sequence, take it slower or read them in their entirety before deciding which days and exercises speak to you. There is no right or wrong way to work through the material; it is an opportunity to lead mindfully in your life in the way that feels best to you.

Leadership and The 28 Days Guidebook Series

Leadership [lee-der-ship]

Noun

1. *the position or function of a leader, a person who guides or directs a group.*
2. *ability to lead*
3. *an act or instance of leading, guidance or direction*

--Dictionary.com

There are two ideas for you to note before engaging with this material.

1. My definition of leadership is different from what people traditionally think about when they envision leaders who are powerfully ensconced in positions of authority. The common definition of leadership references a position or office as the precursor to leadership. In other words, title over personal efficacy—and everyone has examples of people in positions of authority who are not conducting themselves as leaders.

How I think about leadership references the second definition usually provided in dictionaries, which has to do with the capacity to lead. Rather than relying on external titles and qualifications, my definition has to do with the process of how people conduct themselves—that is, are they leading by giving the best of themselves in service to the greater good. A shorthand definition I use is "love in action." True leadership is our natural state, it is whom we are all born to be, leaders in our lives and world: active, engaged participants who are determining the course of our lives. By switching the reference to our internal choice to lead lives of meaning and service, it makes leadership accessible to all of us, all the time.

2. This is the second in a series of leadership guidebooks. I've written these books to be read however, feels best to you and applied to your life immediately. They are intended to be continually referenced throughout your life and leadership journey. Each lesson stands alone and together they provide a guide to become the leader you already are. The first book, *Living the Leadership Choice*, details the proprietary leadership model I've developed to allow people to lead in their work and world. This book, *Choose To Lead*, prepares us in greater depth for the journey to success in the world by fully engaging our inner resources to create the clarity, power and strength to achieve our goals. The next book about Leading in Relationships will be out soon.

Introduction

For twenty-five years, I have been working with individuals to bring out their talents, strengths and passions to create lives of service that are both fulfilling and abundant. Time and again, people find themselves stuck. This is because they don't understand who they are, which makes enjoying the present and creating a vibrant future challenging. Perhaps even more challenging is that successful professionals, particularly those in the political and policy arenas in which I primarily work, find these exercises frightening, not because they are incapable of completing them, rather because the answers to these questions may be divergent from the path they have so rigorously pursued for years.

I fundamentally believe that our highest and best selves want to leave the world a better place. For most of us, from our earliest childhood memories, we longed to bring our talents into the world to make the world better. Doctor, lawyer, firefighter, the archetypal images of a five-year-old hold the foundation of our purpose and the aspirations of our lives; yet, within a few years of imagining and honing the dream, other people entered the picture to tell us it wasn't going to happen. Too dumb, not talented enough, beyond our reach, whatever and whoever it was, the message was clear—you don't get to be who you are, who you KNOW that you are. So we shift, we push, we pursue, and we move forward toward an illusion of what will make us happy and successful, leaving that carefree, content child behind. Before we know it adulthood is upon us, and the consequences of these decisions hit us square in the face.

For example, I once gave a presentation to a top international law firm's partners and associates on how best to present themselves as leaders. Arriving in their museum-quality offices, I anticipated a lively discussion on leadership, authenticity and effective communication as the cornerstone of professional success. While the audience consisted of only a handful of partners, the majority of associates who attended were leaden and morose, reflecting their lifeless surroundings.

My presentations can be considered many things; however, they are not heavy and disengaging. After two hours of effort with little effect, I was feeling less than thrilled with the experience and wondered if their reticence was rooted in their own confusion about the decision that had brought them to that conference room.

One of the younger and slightly more energetic attendees came up to compliment me after the session. In thanking him, I commented that I didn't feel I connected with the audience in the way I usually do during presentations. He said, "Don't worry about it. All these people are here because they are smart and didn't know what to do when college ended, so they applied to law school. And because they are smart and got good grades, they got offers from firms like this that pay them a lot of money to do work they hate. They don't know how to answer the questions you asked and probably wouldn't like the answers if they did." I was floored. Not that I hadn't run across people who didn't know what they wanted to do with their lives; I just couldn't believe that one of the top law firms, for which so many people aspired to work, had so many associates who looked like they would rather be anywhere else other than in their palatial offices.

One might think that this story ends with the tragedy of highly educated and well-paid individuals lost in the world of law. It doesn't. After the presentation, I met with the firm's managing partner. I shared my shock at the lack of enthusiasm and willingness to engage on topics fundamental to successful leadership—even success in general. I suggested, be it me or someone else, it would be relatively easy to meet with the associates to discern whose talents, skills and passions truly aligned with the organization and whose would not. In essence, identify those who fit and would be a true asset to the firm and allow those who will not succeed in the long term to recognize that their talents can be more fully utilized. Make sense? Apparently, not, because he politely said to me, albeit in much nicer terms, he didn't care who fit and who didn't; those who survive stay and for those who didn't he had 12 people in line to replace them. He was voicing a position taken by many organizations that don't care for the individual and only the bottom line.

With examples like this, it is no wonder it is challenging to stay true to your passion and purpose when organizations don't care about supporting your clarity. Companies like this one will use your time and knowledge no differently than those who work on a manufacturing line—that is, in a purely transactional way. This phenomenon exists in all sectors of society, not just prestigious law firms, and is a byproduct of a world that is driven by profit and power, having and holding, rather than service and satisfaction.

The secret truth, however, is that those who lack service to others and the community as a fundamental part of their work find a hollow appeal keeping them trapped in the illusion of power and money and as the be-all and end-all of one's life. Yet, no amount of money, no position of power ever compares to fulfilling work that is aligned with your talents and strengths in service to others. That doesn't mean that those pursuing their passion can't achieve great financial success and impact—it is generally those who are living their passion who are successful and prosperous over the long term. And it doesn't mean that there aren't plenty of people with money and power who are not living their passion—because there are. It means that even in gilded palaces, when you put external motivations ahead of core needs happiness remains elusive.

As an endnote to this tale of woe at one of the nation's elite law firms, within a year of this experience, it had gone bankrupt. Not surprising to those who saw the truth and a reminder that without aligned leaders in an organization, long-term prosperity and success are tenuous. Leadership matters especially when it comes to those who represent the future of any organization—if you don't cultivate leadership within your workforce, your foundation is weak. The same is true for our communities, our nation and the world.

So what can you do to lead, to create change in your life and in your world? Do you need to embark on a journey that will take you around the world? Do you need make it to the corner office? Or be elected President? No. Transformation through leadership comes when you make a conscious decision to live your life differently. The simplicity is beautiful. Leadership begins in the only place where you have the power to create change—within you. Therefore, power, real power, resides within each one of us equally because each one of us has the power to decide how we will lead our lives.

Yet for so many, we too easily give away this power. We let circumstances—other people, situations and the world in general—reflect back and dictate how we "should" be feeling in any moment. We let those external factors tell us whether we are smart or stupid, successful or a failure, rich or poor, etc. Think how different the world would be if each one of us took responsibility for what we were putting OUT into the world instead of feeling powerless about what is coming in. What could each of us do differently if we understood that every action we take, every person we meet, and every situation we are involved with could be different if we chose to do it differently?

Leaders are those people who are willing to accept responsibility for their actions and realize that, through their lives, they can become an inspiration for others to see that same potential in them. **Leadership is not about putting something on, learning a new set of skills, or knowing how to orchestrate others. Leadership is the capacity to live one's life with integrity, openly, honestly and with the willingness to share talents, skills and passions with others to create a community, society and world in which we all want to live**. This means that leaders exist everywhere, not just on the vast stages of political, cultural, and business realms; rather, most leaders are found in classrooms, stores, homes and communities. More often than not, it is these individuals, the "common" players in our lives, who make the ultimate difference. These people first recognize our spark, help us to see it in ourselves,

14

and then coach, teach, mentor and inspire us to move forward with these gifts.

Are you ready to lead? Let's begin.

Two New Concepts for Leadership Development

Remembering Forward

"Remembering Forward" is the term I have coined for living into our true selves. In part, it comes from the idea that if everything we can imagine already exists, it is sometimes easier to create our future if we are "remembering" it as if it already happened; in other words, it takes the questioning out of "if" it will happen because we can only remember things that have already occurred. The other part of the concept evolves from the notion that truly to move forward into the life and world we wish to create; we must remember our essence, who we truly are as a person and as a part of our community and society.

Each one of us has three components to how we present ourselves to the world. There is the part of ourselves that is created by our memories and experience in the past; there is the person we are in the moment; and there are our hopes and dreams, our potential for the future. This framework is detailed in numerous books, and my favorite is Bryan Hubbard's "The Untrue Story of You." In sum, the only place you have any control is in the present moment, and yet so many of our actions are based on stories from the past and anxieties about the future. Until we come clear about what is in the moment and what we are bringing forward, we often cede our power, and our leadership, to circumstances and conditions that don't exist or never will.

On the other hand, we can use the device of our ego to choose to create what we want instead of allowing stories and thoughts of what we don't desire to run the show. Remembering forward allows us to choose the best of what we bring to the moment and create what we want rather than allowing our lives to be governed by circumstances "beyond our control." Everything in this moment is within your control and in that is the power to change your world. Remember from a perspective of choice and empowerment and it allows you to create what you desire, not what you fear.

Understanding your power is difficult. Believing you have it is almost beyond comprehension, but you are a powerful creator of your reality. As Marianne Williamson states, "Our greatest fear is not that we are powerless, it is that we are powerful beyond belief." It is far easier to point the finger at others as the reason for your despair, rather than to recognize that you alone have the power to shift the situation. Because once you have accepted that, you are the one making the choices in your life—you then become fully responsible for the choices you are making. Are you sad? Frustrated? What are you doing to contribute to those feelings? Emotions are great signs and indicators of alignment in your life. Negative emotions offer you an opportunity to ask yourself, what choices can I be making to feel the way I want to feel? In other words, once you realize that you really are the center of the Universe, you acknowledge it is your own thoughts and actions that create the world in which you live.

You are not alone in having things in your past that have been hurtful, traumatic and painful. For most, they see themselves and remember the experience as a victim, traumatized and in pain carrying the hurt forward. The choice, the leadership, in remembering forward is to choose to see yourself as someone who experienced great hurt, who figured out a way through and who has created new opportunities. If the belief is, *I can take a tough situation and make it better*, then the belief you remember forward is, *I am strong and able to handle challenges easily.* The best part of this phenomenon is that in trusting in your strength, the problems become fewer and your ability to handle them less stressful, because in remembering correctly, you can and will make it through.

Each day during the 28-Day *Choose to Lead* exercises, you will review events from your life and have the opportunity to remember forward. These exercises will create a new story of your life and open up new options for your future. When you create a cohesive story line that resonates with the person, you are today and where you want to be tomorrow, life shifts in unimagined ways.

What if There is Nothing Wrong With You?

Wrong. The word itself doesn't even feel good to say or write, and yet for so many of us, it is the underpinning of our entire existence. What is wrong with me? How can I fix it? How long will it take me to fix it so that I can have what I want? Or be happy? I doubt there is a human being alive on this planet who has not experienced this inner dialogue—and what a shame that this is the way in which so many of us come to see and exist in the world. A world where everyone else is smarter, prettier, better, wealthier, and until we can figure out what keeps us in our "less than" state, we are doomed to our present life.

In addition to Remembering Forward, in this 28-day course, I introduce a second powerful concept to guide you in becoming a leader in your life. To move forward in the moment and into the future fully empowered in being you, it is imperative that everyone fully believes in him or herself. Without that belief, we create roadblocks to putting our leadership into the world. Everyone wants a clear path and using the question, *what if there is nothing wrong with you,* is the easiest way to make it so.

Ask yourself, *what...if...there...is...nothing...wrong... with...me?* Take just a moment and sit with that thought and the temptation to find something "wrong" and then just erase it. WOW! In the first moments of pondering this thought, were you, like me, uncharacteristically speechless? For me, not only was the thought completely freeing, but it gave way to the realization that my life has been spent believing that who I am, somehow, is flawed and requires a relentless search for appeasement, atonement, forgiveness and change. Somehow, I wholeheartedly bought into the idea that I needed fixing to have all that I really wanted — and that if I don't have it, then something needs to be fixed! Have you been feeling the same way? How different life would be if nothing needed fixing, and moving toward goals

19

could come from a place of solidity and wholeness, entirely open to all possibilities of creating whatever we desired. Hard to believe and hardly the way most of us are living.

After experiencing this slate-cleaning experience, I started asking clients, friends, and colleagues, "What if nothing is wrong with you?" Their responses elicited, as you would suspect, the same reaction —a long silence followed by "Wow, I am not sure I know how to answer that question." Subsequent responses came in various waves from, "Then I have wasted a lot of money on therapy," to "I would live my life very differently." Both true and reflective of the spectrum ranging from "There is something I am doing wrong" to the possibility that "I am limitless" — which, oh by the way, scares the heck out of most people!

So, before reading any further, answer this question: If there were nothing wrong with you, what WOULD you do? Not what COULD you accomplish, but what WOULD you accomplish? What WOULD your life look like and how WOULD you feel? Using "could" sends you right back into the thoughts of what is wrong with me, what am I lacking, ambition, time, money...the belief that gets brought to the surface is I am inadequate....period. That is not a good feeling, is it? Using "would," however, takes you on a journey to being YOU, whole-hearted, authentic, nothing is wrong with me YOU.

When you embrace the idea that nothing is wrong with you, the barriers to being all that you already are and living in the world each day disappear. As your visions for a limitless future dance through your head, you may perhaps realize that you have designed your entire identity around SOMETHING IS WRONG WITH ME. Let it go, find space for the belief that in fact, everything is exactly just the way that it is -- not right, not wrong, not good, not bad. Let go of fighting yourself, of being your own worst enemy, and instead take action that moves you on with your life without the debilitating drag of believing that you have to fix something or someone (yourself and others) all the time. "It is what it is" seems to be the new mantra for putting up with an unwanted reality, but it doesn't help you feel better about yourself, your job, your marriage, your kids, your illnesses or your existence in your world. Leadership becomes the way to be your best and in turn create the best in the world—not a surrender of responsibility, rather surrendering to being the best of yourself and creating a world from a place of trust.

This book is a guide through the process of rooting out this belief in your life and is really about accepting that who are you in this moment is enough to be, do, have and live any way, anything, and anyhow you desire. There is nowhere you need to go, nothing you need to become and certainly nothing else to do other than to accept and love who you are. Then you will be able to project THAT you, the newly appreciated, -recognized and - authentic you, forward into the world.

The 28-Day Choose To Lead Guidebook

Understanding the Process

The Format for the 28 Days

Day of the Week: The course includes four seven-day weeks, beginning with Monday. Each day corresponds to various parts of the body, mind and spirit, and they will be described here.

Quote: A quote will lead you into the lesson for the day.

Defining Question and/or Theme: Each day there is a question or theme that will provide the lesson or learning.

Remembering Forward—How it works in the world: Remembering forward is how we anchor our true selves into the life we are creating. This section will guide you through how to do that with each day's lesson.

Quote: The second quote will help illuminate the path others have taken on this journey.

Mantra: This is a phrase for you to repeat throughout the day to anchor the learning and understanding into your life.

Practice what if there is nothing wrong with you: We know there is nothing wrong with you, and by putting this concept into practice with each day's insights; you are grounding these lessons in the power of you.

From My Experience: This section provides examples and anecdotes from my and my client's experiences to illuminate the day's lesson.

The 28 Days

1st Monday: How Will The World Be Different As A Result Of My Being Here?

1st Tuesday: Who Am I?

1st Wednesday: What Do I Desire?

1st Thursday: What Is My Passion?

1st Friday: What Do I Bring To Relationships?

1st Saturday: How Can I Serve?

1st Sunday: What Is The World Showing Me About My Life?

2nd Monday: What Is My Contribution?

2nd Tuesday: What Are My Unique Talents And Skills?

2nd Wednesday: What Qualities Do I Look For In Others?

2nd Thursday: What Are My Archetypes?

2nd Friday: What Are The Best Qualities I Express In Relationships?

2nd Saturday: What Is The Purpose In What I Do?

2nd Sunday: How Do I Feel When I Have A Peak Experience?

3rd Monday: How Do I Offer My Gifts? Acknowledge Others?

3rd Tuesday: How Do I Make Choices? Where Do I Feel It In My Body?

3rd Wednesday: How Do I Practice Acceptance? Responsibility? Defenselessness?

3rd Thursday: How Do I Balance Desire With The Present Moment?

3rd Friday: How Do I Detach From Outcome And Accept Uncertainty?

3rd Saturday: How Do I Connect Service To The (Natural) World?

3rd Sunday: How Do I Integrate Silence, Nature And Non-Judgment Into My Life?

4th Monday: Using My Leadership Skills

4th Tuesday: Communicating Who I Am

4th Wednesday: Being Clear About What I Want

4th Thursday: Using Your Passion as Power

4th Friday: Creating Community

4th Saturday: Taking Action

4th Sunday: The Upward Spiral

1st Monday: Beginning in the Heart

Know who you are and what makes you unique. All you need to lead is to be your best and to freely share it with the world—
Kathleen Schafer

How Will the World Be Different as a Result of My Being Here?

Every person has something unique to offer the world. While our talents and strengths come to us naturally, it is up to each person to decide on what to focus, what to hone and what to practice — and then to take action to make it happen. If we anchor our actions in clarity about the impact we wish to have on our world, our lives become congruent with whom we are and flow the way they are intended to ~~do so~~. We don't have to struggle or fight to be heard, recognized or included, because once we express our true nature and are clear about the impact we wish to have on the world, the next step becomes clear — and all we have to do is take it.

Remembering Forward—How it Works in the World:
Remember a time when you felt clear and certain in your being—a time when, who you are, was good enough. Use that feeling today to bring your awareness to the impact you are having on every situation in which you are involved. Are you bringing your best? Will the people in this interaction be better off because of it? Will the world be different in the ways you want as a result?

When I ask clients what is the change they wish to see in the world, people almost always go back to the basics: more love, greater respect, equity and opportunity for all. Ask yourself this question and then remember forward—remember what you want for the world and then act to create in in your world each day.

29

I am Me. In all the world, there is no one else exactly like me. Everything that comes out of me is authentically mine, because I alone chose it—I own everything about me: my body, my feelings, my mouth, my voice, all my actions, whether they be to others or myself. I own my fantasies, my dreams, my hopes, my fears. I own my triumphs and successes, all my failures and mistakes. Because I own all of me, I can become intimately acquainted with me. By so doing, I can love me and be friendly with all my parts. I know there are aspects about myself that puzzle me, and other aspects that I do not know -- but as long as I am friendly and loving to myself, I can courageously and hopefully look for solutions to the puzzles and ways to find out more about me. However, I look and sound, whatever I say and do, and whatever I think and feel at a given moment in time is authentically me. If later some parts of how I looked, sounded, thought, and felt turn out to be unfitting, I can discard that which is unfitting, keep the rest, and invent something new for that which I discarded. I can see, hear, feel, think, say, and do. I have the tools to survive, to be close to others, to be productive, and to make sense and order out of the world of people and things outside of me. I own me, and therefore, I can engineer me. I am me, and I am Okay—**Virginia Satir**

Mantra: *The world will be different because I am here, because each day I _____.*

Practice What if There is Nothing Wrong with You: Today stay centered in your heart and feel the unique contribution that only you can bring to the world. What is the power that lies dormant in you? Identify it by day's end and share it with at least one person.

From My Experience: One of the greatest challenges people face when beginning the leadership journey is overcoming the belief that they need to become something they are not. Most of us have come to believe that we need to learn, shift, or change who we are to become the person we want to be and live the life we desire. The focus is outward, the quest unending and unrelentingly frustrating.

Early in my career, I aspired to mold myself like the political leaders I saw on the news each day. It was a time when there were few women political leaders and the atmosphere even more masculine than today. As I entered the political world I felt I had to be a tough fighter to succeed—a view that was reinforced through my experiences. I developed a take-no-prisoner approach to my work and succeeded in many ways. Yet the victories came at a cost. In basing my success on external conquests, I lost me. I gave up balance, openness and joy and became brittle, tired and weary.

Once I realized there was a different way to lead, I found myself angry that I had let so much time pass "doing it the wrong way." Moreover, that feeling was only more of the same pattern, looking externally for reasons to justify how I felt.

The truth is that who we are in this moment is perfect. All these experiences brought me to the beginning of a journey to living more of who I was. I couldn't change them, but I could change what I would do next. I understood that if I had the courage to unearth the real me, then I could create the life and have the impact I yearned for. This has made all the difference for me— by focusing on how I wanted to feel each day as I made my contribution to the world, the creation of external results became a much easier and successful process.

I have a unique ability —and desire— to understand other people, their motivations + fears, and help others become more empathetic to them as a result.
—I just don't always use my powers for good. :

1st Tuesday: Creating a Strong Foundation

The unexamined life is not worth living—**Socrates**

Who Am I?

Who am I? A simple question that is often answered with a description of the trappings of the external world—roles, titles, achievements, and possessions. Yet, none of these things is actually YOU. YOU are the being that identifies with these descriptors—the roles, titles, achievements and possessions. Feeling confident in your power comes from knowing that who you are is greater than what you do, where you live or how much money you make. Because once you understand that who you are is remarkable, genius, unique and full of talents and strengths the world needs, no one can take that away from you—unless you allow them to do so. The greatness of who you are remains unchanged while the external reflection of that may come and go. The choice is yours: look outside to access your worth, or go inside and connect to your true power to guide you through the outside world.

Remembering Forward—How It Works in the World: The conversation about believing in one's uniqueness and being valuable often brings up misgivings about trusting that it is true when: I just lost my job, my boss never allows me to spearhead a project, my girlfriend just left me, etc. While each situation is different and complex, without exception, one constant remains if we are honest: in not being our best selves, we play a part in creating the difficult situation. Regardless whether we are our true selves or not, we are the creators of our world, not other people. If we take responsibility for creating our world, people who are harsh to us can only do so when there is a part of us that already believes the same things to be true. The world will reflect our negative self-judgment back to us. Use difficult situations to understand where your negative self-talk is lurking.

In remembering forward today, reflect on situations that didn't have the results you wanted and remember them as they could have been—with you as your best self, the person you truly are. Then remember forward toward your next meeting, job, relationship, etc., and envision being your best self and experience how different you feel.

> *And I don't want the world to see me*
> *'Cause I don't think that they'd understand*
> *When everything's made to be broken*
> *I want you to know who I am—**Who I Am**,* **Goo Goo Dolls**

Mantra: *Knowing who I am and being my best allows me to create the life I want to live.*

Practice What if There is Nothing Wrong with You: As you begin your day, write down the three qualities that you feel best describe YOU. As you go about your day, ask five other people to share the three qualities they feel best describe you. Reflect on the similarities and differences among the lists and allow yourself to own your best qualities, letting go of so-called "weaknesses" and living as if there is nothing wrong with you.

From My Experience: Clients often begin working with me when something has triggered feelings of unworthiness in them. Being passed over for a promotion or leadership role, a relationship crisis or consistently missed opportunities to do "more" with their lives create a desire to change. Interestingly, they soon realize that although one area of their life may have triggered our discussion, there are similar issues at play in all areas of their lives.

Usually within our first hour together two things become clear. The first is that there is a false, or limiting belief, they have about themselves, such as, "no one listens to what I have to say," or "I don't get what I want." The second is that the truth of who each person is, is powerful. I am constantly in awe of my clients, who they are as individuals and what they have to offer the world.

During our initial time together, I focus on guiding people to see the truth of who they are and it is a two-step practice. Rid people of the beliefs that are "less than" and focus on the unique talents and strengths of who they are. It is a symbiotic and vital practice for everyone everyday—release what is false and lead from the power of who you are. This is the foundation of leading. By living from your strength, you shift every area of your life.

1st Wednesday: Desires Fuel Passion

We are desire. It is the essence of the human soul, the secret of our existence. Absolutely nothing of human greatness is ever accomplished without it. Not a symphony has been written, a mountain climbed, an injustice fought, or a love sustained apart from desire. Desire fuels our search for the life we prize. Our desire, if we listen to it, will save us from committing soul-suicide, the sacrifice of our hearts on the altar of "getting by." The same old thing is not enough. It never will be—**John Eldredge, *Desire***

What Do I Desire?

Sacrificing our hearts on the altar of "getting by," a powerful sentiment and, sadly, one that far too many of us can relate to. How often do we observe our family, friends and colleagues getting by? Is it a co-worker who is miserable in his job but just can't leave the benefits? Perhaps it is a friend whose marriage is in tatters and yet feels trapped by society and the stigma of a "broken home." Or it may be a sibling who has never been able to live up to the family's expectations? Whatever the situation, the gap between what we desire and what we have is often so great, because we are focused on "the way it looks" rather than "how it feels."

Wanting is about things. Desires are about feelings. Wants are external to ourselves; desires are internal. When we focus on external wants, we are always in lack; when we identify what we truly desire, we find that the power to create rests in one place— within ourselves. If we have the power to fulfill our desires now, attracting our wants into our lives becomes a habitual, everyday experience.

Remembering Forward—How It Works in the World: As children, our wants are simple: to be fed, cleaned, held, loved. As we grow, we are introduced into the world of desire—strongly wishing for something, be it a colorful block with which our

37

friend is playing, another bite of chocolate pudding or our mother's sole focus and attention as the lens through which we ascertain how we feel. In so doing, we are immediately presented with the reality that others do not always meet our desires. Therefore, along with the desire to use external things to feel good, comes the reality that they aren't always fulfilled by others the ways our basic wants once were. Through this process, we allow those first experiences to reflect into us a belief that we don't deserve to have our desires fulfilled, because as children we came to believe that power rested with the adults in our lives. The ability to satisfy our desires becomes arrested and the focus for their fulfillment placed on other people being the gatekeeper to our satisfaction.

As adults, we can shift this pattern. Take a few quiet moments and remember forward for today, what would it feel like to live the entire day *knowing* your desires are met? Next, play with the idea that for each day your desires are met, a further spring of desire emerges, anew, and as you savor it, you know that it will manifest and the process will start yet again. Remember forward to a life filled with the creation and completion of experiencing desire, its obtainment and knowing it's an unending process.

Desire animates the world. It is present in the baby crying for milk, the girl struggling to solve a math problem, the woman running to meet her lover and later deciding to have children, and the old woman, hunched over her walker, moving down the hall of the nursing home at glacial pace to pick up her mail. Banish desire from the world and you get a world of frozen beings who have no reason to live and no reason to die— **William Braxton Irvine, *On Desire***

Mantra: *Desire animates my world and my desires are met with grace and ease.*

Practice What if There is Nothing Wrong With You: Often the reason we feel our desires will not be met is because we believe there is something fundamentally wrong with us—that was the original reason we felt we didn't deserve the extra bite of chocolate pudding or our mother's singular focus. This is a deeply embedded pattern and one of which it is time to be free. There is nothing wrong with you. Who you are in this moment is reason enough to have every desire fulfilled—you deserve unconditional love, joy, abundance and happiness in your life.

Write a list of all the reasons you don't deserve to have your desires met. Then find the common thread(s) in the list and resolve to release them from your life. Start by physically ridding yourself of the list: burn it, bury it, and throw it away. Whatever you do today, do it with the intention that you will free yourself of the barriers that have been keeping you from experiencing your desires.

From My Experience: At the end of the day, everyone wants to feel happy and fulfilled. While we may create circumstances, conditions and other means of evaluating our happiness, ultimately it is our greatest desire. With happiness as the goal is it incredible how many people unconsciously erect barriers to experiencing it.

If you don't have what you want in your life or you have things that you don't want, the only person responsible is YOU. It is a maddening and freeing concept. In working with clients, the limiting belief becomes clear by finding the disconnect between what they are saying they want and what they are actually doing.

For example, if someone says they want to enjoy their work and yet are showing up every day dissatisfied with their co-workers, angry with their boss and unenthusiastic with their work, it isn't a mystery why they aren't happy. By harnessing the power of choice, a key leadership practice, the person recognizes all the choices *they* are making that are creating the unwanted. He or she can choose to find value in their work and with their colleagues that may shift any number of factors that will concretely shift the experience, not only for them, for those around them as well—now that's leadership.

Understanding our desire takes us to the heart of a core leadership practice—conscious choice. That is, YOU are choosing every experience in your life, you are deciding how you are thinking and feeling about it and you are making choice about the actions you will and will not take as a result. There is nothing more powerful than a person who understands through his or her choices that they are creating their reality.

Therefore, the identification of our true desires starts you on this process by putting the focus on what matters most to you. When you are clear about what you desire then all your actions start to line-up to support realizing them. Once you do that, it is a very short time before you start experiencing real world results—and feeling happier too. I've seen miraculous changes in people and their lives once they go through this process and embrace it as a way to live and lead throughout their lives.

1st Thursday: Passion and Clarity

There is no passion to be found playing small – in settling for a life that is less than the one you are capable of living—**Nelson Mandela**

What is My Passion?

Passion is the spark that ignites our fire, and our fire is what fuels our lives. We are a society that has insisted on drowning the fires of passion in pursuit of a life that meets conventional norms. We have backed away from our passion because, for most of us, early in our lives someone communicated, and we believed, that our pursuits weren't worthy or didn't meet someone else's (or society's) standard of success.

Yet, the dirty little secret about passion is that without it, no amount of success will ever fill the hole left by the lack of it in your life. Time and again, I work with people who are at the top levels of success in their careers, professionally and financially, who are unhappy with the quality of their lives. Passion is what's missing. Ask most people what they are passionate about and moments of silence will often be followed by "What does that have to do with being successful?" or "I don't know, does it really matter?" Yes, it does. No longer will success "outside" come easily or as fruitfully if we are not tuned to our passions and able to create a life that fully integrates them.

Remembering Forward—How It Works in the World: The question I often ask my clients is, "When you were five years old, what did you want to be when you grew up?" While the dreams of a young child may not be totally indicative of a future life's work, it does contain the seeds of the dream, the passion. Teachers, astronauts, firefighters, doctors—there were reasons these professions appealed to you. Was it the order and excitement of the classroom? Was it the ability to make people feel better or rescue them from a threatening situation?

41

Whatever the genesis of that passion it made you, YOU—that being who was excited by the possibilities that still exists in you. Take a moment and feel into what that dream felt like when you were five years old. Can you feel the possibilities? The excitement? The enthusiasm? The passion? Now think about your life today. Is the passion there? If not, identify the first time you felt your flame being doused by another's cold bucket of water. Recognize the choices you made to step away from your passion and resolve to remember forward into the passion that once existed, the passion that is your true nature. Look for at least one way today to express your passion and remember forward into each new situation of bringing that passionate five-year-old with you.

Rest in reason; move in passion—**Khalil Gibran**

Mantra: *My passion animates my life and I am passionate about* _____*.*

Practice What if There is Nothing Wrong with You: What if there is nothing wrong with pursuing your passion? Do you love to cook? Perhaps your passion is to be in nature or to work with the aging. Whatever your passion, start living from this moment forward as if there is nothing wrong with pursuing it, because there isn't. As a part of your commitment to living your passions, find time each week to make an appointment with yourself to start integrating your passion into your life. After years of neglecting your passions, they won't come magically roaring into your life, transforming you instantaneously. By staying committed to living a life based on your passions, you will shift the landscape of your life—sometimes with the subtle force of water wearing down rock and at other times with the seismic shift of an earthquake. In whatever way the shifts occur, embrace and appreciate them and know that you deserve to live a life of passion; indeed, it is the only life worth living.

From My Experience: I love feeling passionate—that sense of excitement, presence, knowing and clarity that comes from engaging in activities that feel good doing them. How wonderful

42

it is to experience a sense of freedom and unlimited potential. I never feel more alive than when I am with people, one-on-one or in groups, talking about leading. While my work has a common thread of guiding people in being their best, everything I do does not fully engage my passion; I still have to oversee accounting, review contracts, etc. However, in knowing what my passion is, each of these tasks has been easier because I see them as a part of being able to practice my passion.

The idea that passion is something that can, and absolutely should, exist in our daily lives is revolutionary for most people. Too often, passion is thought to be that experience that exists outside of our work, rather than the fuel for lives filled with leadership and meaning. When we harness our passion, our life changes. We find new meaning in the things in which we are currently engaged and we find new ways to put our leadership into the world to serve others. The greatest gift in passion is that it shows us where our leadership is needed. When we answer the call, the reward is more and more opportunity to lead passionately.

When I started following my passion the path changed—and sometimes it was challenging not knowing exactly where I was headed. What I've found after practicing passionate leadership is that I know that the only time I've been lost is when I stopped following my passion; it is a misstep I now make with much less frequency. By staying attuned to what feels good, I make clear choices and lead from a more powerful place.

1st Friday: Leading Relationships

*If civilization is to survive, we must cultivate the science of human relationships—the ability of all peoples, of all kinds, to live together, in the same world at peace—***Franklin Roosevelt**

What Do I Bring to Relationships?

The word "relationship" brings to mind personal connections while "leadership" is often reserved for how we conduct ourselves in our professional or "outside" lives. Relationships are frequently taken for granted, and leadership is something for ambitious people in corner offices. In my work, leadership is about how we conduct ourselves in relationships, whether personal or professional. And to be the most effective in our lives, it is essential to lead ourselves in every relationship by being our best, bringing our talents and strengths to the table, being clear about our needs and desires and allowing other people to do the same.

When we apply this broader definition of leadership, the patterns of our individual behavior become clear, for we cannot be someone with our colleagues and be someone entirely different with our family or vice versa. True leadership is authentic, which means it doesn't change in different situations—the essence is ever-present. Without exception, the challenges one faces in personal or professional situations are at their core the same because the person is the same.

Remembering Forward—How It Works in the World: What are the three consistent qualities you bring to your relationships? Write down your thoughts and spend time today reflecting on the impact they have on your relationships. If you feel you are "caring," what does it mean to you? How are others experiencing it? In the answer to this question lies the key to every relationship problem, that is, what one person perceives as a positive quality can be experienced by another as a challenge. For example, what one person perceives as organized, another might find stifling and over structured.

Try this exercise: close your eyes and mentally draw a circle around you. As you stand inside the circle, see the positive qualities you bring to relationships inside the circle with you; feel the gifts you have to offer others. Next, envision someone with whom your relationship is currently positive, see him or her coming up to the circle, and allow him or her to receive your gifts as he or she chooses to do so. Witness what that looks and feels like to you. Next, envision someone with whom you are experiencing some challenges in your relationship and see him or her walk up to your circle. Can you allow him or her to receive your gifts based on his or her needs, or do you feel yourself needing to push your wishes or strengths on him or her? Feel the difference in you as you allow the other person to accept your gifts as they are best for him or her, not how you feel they are best. Leadership is about standing firm in your best and allowing others to engage, or not, as feels best for them.

In remembering forward today, practice the feeling of being clear about what you bring to relationships, rooting into your strengths and allowing others the choice as to how to engage with you and your strengths. Remember how it feels to be yourself, free of needing to change or shift others, and then walk in the freedom of simply being you in all your relationships.

Our greatest joy and our greatest pain comes in our relationships with others—**Stephen Covey**

Mantra: *Who I am is the greatest gift I offer in every relationship.*

Practice what if there is nothing wrong with you: Deepak Chopra says, "Flaws are really the scars and hurts accumulated over a lifetime." We are trained to see the flaws in others and the flaws in ourselves—amplifying the hurt, everyone has experienced, because flaws are the untruths we believe about others and ourselves. Yet the greatest gift you have to offer anyone in a relationship is the unique you. If you want to do one thing that will change your life in the most dramatic way in the least amount of time, stop berating yourself for your flaws and stop doing it to others.

This doesn't mean there is nothing more to learn, or new ways to grow; it simply means that focusing on the pain only exacerbates it. Today your practice is to lead your life as if there is nothing wrong with you—and to treat everyone you interact with as if the exact same thing is true for him or her. Write down your reflections at the end of the day.

From My Experience: Owning that who we are is enough to be loved, happy and successful is a tough pill to swallow. Because we often focus on the lack of these experiences in our life, we want to be able to believe there is something we can do to bring it into our lives. This fodder keeps a billion-dollar self-help industry in full swing.

The difference between helping ourselves and leading in our lives is the difference on the focus between what's wrong with you and what's right. In reading and practicing self-help methods, I may have felt better for a short period, but ultimately I ended up where I started—focusing on the issue that brought me there to begin with. The "ah-ha" moment for me was when I realized that the balanced leadership I was teaching people to pursue in politics wasn't going to take root until I realized the power of what I had to bring to others just as I was. I didn't need to be on a Presidential campaign to show my work had value; rather I had to value my work so that, hopefully, one day someone will pursue the Presidency guided by this leadership model. In the meantime, thousands of others have benefitted from this work and I have no doubt one of them will become President.

1st Saturday: Serving Others

I slept and dreamt that life was joy. I awoke and saw that life was service. I acted and behold, service was joy—**Rabindranath Tagore**

How Can I Serve?

This quote is in the signature line of one of my favorite people in the world. She has graced the covers of fashion magazines, won awards for her work in movies, negotiated peace in some of the world's most difficult regions and has worked tirelessly to protect and propagate the wisdom of indigenous populations throughout the world. To look at her without knowing her accomplishments, one would never expect to discover the treasure trove of experiences that make up her life. Yet, that is true for most of us. While we may not have achieved the same heights, we have walked a path unique to us; it is our story, and without exception, our success and happiness directly correlate to how we use our talents and strengths to serve others.

For those who choose the road less traveled, following passion and finding joy means looking beyond the external trappings of success and surrendering to the guidance that shows us the way, simply by feeling its rightness for us in the moment. Don't we all dream of a life of joy? Too often, we believe that life comes from appearing on the covers of magazines or winning awards instead of from where it really comes. The truth is joy comes from service to others and *knowing* that using our talents and strengths to enrich the lives of others is the only way to live contentedly. From that place of balance comes the ability to create whatever level of abundance we desire.

Remembering Forward—How It Works in the World:

Can you remember a time when you spontaneously helped another human being? A Facebook friend recently wrote about grabbing an elderly man out of oncoming traffic. Other clients and friends have shared about offering a few extra dollars to a person in line who doesn't have the money to pay for their food, or a smile and word of kindness offered to a woman crying in the restroom. Whatever you did that helped another, allow yourself a moment to connect to that feeling. It is special in a way no other emotion resonates; helping another to whom we have no connection, for the simple reason of being kind creates joy.

While continuing to feel into that experience, allow yourself to expand the thought to the moments when you used your talents and strengths in the same way. Did you make a meal with love that changed someone's day? Were you able to figure out a tough legal problem that helped a group of people? Or perhaps you raised money and goods to support people in crisis. Whatever you did to offer the best of yourself in service, I know it felt good to you. This feeling is the amazing fuel for your life. As you go through your day, remember forward; allow that feeling to guide you to opportunities to put your best self to work in the world. There are so many more opportunities, and as you remember forward and take the next step, many more will continue to find you.

The best way to find yourself is to lose yourself in service to others—**Mahatma Gandhi**

Mantra: *Joy comes from doing what I love in service to others.*

Practice What if There is Nothing Wrong with You: If joy comes from using our talents in service to others, why aren't we all doing it? Two keys reasons constantly arise in my leadership work with clients: one, people can't identify their talents and strengths or how they want to serve others; and two, they don't believe they can do what they love in service to others and make a living. How sad it is that so many of us shy away from our happiness out of fear that who we are isn't going to work in the world.

Go back to that feeling of joy that comes from serving others — there is nothing wrong with that, and it is your starting point.

How can you take one-step today to create more of those opportunities in your life? What can you do to evoke that same feeling? Perhaps in a smaller version and today, resolve to do at least one thing that will create the same dynamic.

There is nothing wrong with you; your talents and strengths will not only bring you joy, they will also bring it to others as well. The only thing keeping you from sharing your gifts with others is you. By practicing "what if there is nothing wrong with you," you can see how those isolated incidents were not haphazard blips in your life, rather they were the markers to show you where to go. Follow those markers and take one-step at a time.

From My Experience: The best part of focusing on bringing more joy into your life is that it is contagious. Not only does one joyful experience lead to others, it ruthlessly spreads to those around you. Incorporate joyful experiences based on service to others in your life and you've found a recipe for many more unexpected pleasures.

Even when I am not officially on the job, be it volunteering, with friends or as a part of various communities, my talents are called forth to guide individuals and groups to lead. Often these experiences are challenging because the stated need is different from the actual desire to lead and navigating them has been difficult. Without a doubt, I've learned tremendous lessons that enriched me, allowed me to do my work with greater insight, and in the process, allowed others to grow as well. Each person, sharing their gifts, elevates the communities in which we live and work and opens the door to joy for everyone. Leadership goes on all the time and when we offer it with joy, we bring that aspect to all those with whom we interact as well.

1st Sunday: What's My Potential?

You are a part of every event that has ever happened, is happening now or ever will happen. You know who you are and what your purpose is. There is no confusion or conflict with any other person on earth. Your purpose in life is to help creation expand and grow—**Deepak Chopra**

What is Happening in my External World? What Are These Things Showing Me About What is Going on Inside of Me?

"When we realize that our true Self is one of pure potential, we align with the power that manifests everything in the universe," says Deepak Chopra. This state of self-referral, our true state, is beyond the opinions or reflection of others. It is immune to criticism, fears and challenges. Look around at what is showing up in your life: is it chaotic, stressful or tense? Or is it peaceful, playful and joyful? Whatever is happening on your outside is a reflection of what is going on with you inside. You are infinite and full of potential to create what you desire—in fact, you are creating it, whether you are aware of it or not. By examining what is already happening in your world, you will not only find clues to what is going on in your inner world, you will discover an amazing truth—that you have the power to create, so it is time to lead and create what you want, not what you don't want.

Once we experience the connection between our inner state and our outer world, the doorway to our leadership opens. With this awareness, we not only see how we create our world, we experience the interconnectedness of all humans and the power of one to impact the whole. For with a shift in you, your outer world changes and with that change is the impact on everyone with whom you come into contact. Therefore, everyone has the capacity to change the world—leaders are the ones who are conscious of this fact and practice it daily with great care. For one's actions never are solitary and being our best is important for our lives and the lives of those around us.

Remembering Forward—How It Works in the World:
Synchronicity is the powerful experience of improbable or
random events occurring in a way that captures your attention.
You are wishing for a few extra hours to finish a project and
suddenly your afternoon meeting is cancelled, or you need to
make a connection with a company when a new employee walks
in to introduce herself and you discover she did an internship
there. These are synchronistic events and they are happening all
around you, all the time. The key to harness this power is to pay
attention and observe the connection you have with the whole.
When you ask for something, it will appear, perhaps not in the
same clear ways as the above examples because it may come in
the form of an idea, a desire to visit some place new or simply
the thought to break from your routine. In pursuing those
insights, one often finds the next breadcrumb on the path.
Leaders learn to connect to their inner desires, "ask" for what
they want *and* participate in its co-creation by staying present to
the synchronicities that occur in their lives.

Remember forward today by looking back on those
synchronistic events that changed your life. A missed plane that
resulted in meeting a future business partner, a desire to go to a
different coffee shop where an old friend sat, or the impulsive
conference you attended that changed your life; whatever the
experiences, marvel at how the unexpected conspired to move
you along your path toward your desires. Harness that feeling of
wonder and allow yourself today to focus on all the tiny
synchronicities that exist every day. As you become mindful of
these small wonders, and are grateful for them, you will quickly
see them grow in your life.

*The rule is jam tomorrow and jam yesterday--but never jam today.
It MUST come sometimes to "jam today,"* Alice objected.

No, it can't, said the Queen. *It's jam every OTHER day, today isn't
any OTHER day, you know.*

I don't understand you, said Alice. *It's dreadfully confusing!*

That's the effect of living backwards, the Queen said kindly. *It always makes one a little giddy at first.*

Living backwards! Alice repeated in great astonishment. *I never heard of such a thing.*

However, there's great advantage in it, that one's memory works both ways, said the Queen.

I'm sure MINE only works one way, Alice remarked. *I can't remember things before they happen.*

It's a poor sort of memory that only works backwards, the Queen remarked—**Lewis Carrol, *Through the Looking Glass***

Mantra: *My life is full of possibilities; I am the creator of my world.*

Practice what if there is nothing wrong with you: Practice silence in your interactions today. Notice the power of not speaking. Observe the compulsive urges to "go out," check your messages or peruse the Internet. How different would your day be if you spent quiet time connecting with yourself, being creative, and being in nature? It is Sunday, the one day of the week when the outside world expects the least from you. Today, give yourself the gift of silence, of connection to that which lies beyond the physical world and the power of your infinite self.

Often we feel the need to connect as our way to stay relevant in the world. By practicing "what if there is nothing wrong with you," you give yourself permission to unplug, to be yourself and know that whatever is important to you will be there waiting and those things that aren't will gradually fade away—and there is nothing wrong with them either.

From My Experience: In my youth and early adulthood, I was known as a whirling dervish—in perpetual motion. I tackled to-do lists, organized every group I engaged with and pushed forward. I loved all the activities and felt I was making the most out of life.

It wasn't until shortly after the birth of my son that I realized the power of silence and its companion stillness. What the silence provided was the space to realize that the activity was fueled by my distrust in life. I didn't believe that things would work out or that synchronicity would be my friend, I believed I had to do it on my own.

As you end you first week, reflect on the changes in you. The shifts you have made simply by turning inward and recognizing your beauty, power and strength. And in so doing, hopefully you are beginning to see that you are not alone in the world needing to make things happen—that indeed your closest ally has been with you all along, that is, your true self.

When we use silence to connect to our true selves we find that trust becomes easier, synchronicity more commonplace and our power to lead in the world unstoppable.

2nd Monday: What Contribution Am I Here to Make?

You're happiest while you're making the greatest contribution—
Robert F. Kennedy

What's My Contribution?

Everyone on this planet has a contribution to make — to themselves, their family and friends, their community, society and the world. You are making this contribution whether you are aware of it or not; the difference between leaders and others is that leaders understand their contribution and use it to guide their actions. If you are unaware of the contribution you are here to make, then your ability to do it well is diminished, and so is your potential for happiness and having the impact you wish to have on the world.

People attempt to unearth their contribution by asking what they want to have accomplished by the end of their lives. This exercise is helpful, yet it often leaves us dreaming of grand accomplishments and removes us from the reality of what we can do now to make our contribution. I ask audiences and clients, "Why are you here?" In other words, why are you at this seminar? This job? Are you here simply to take things away, i.e., information, compensation, etc., or are you here to offer something? If you want to be a leader in your life, focusing on the contribution first takes care of the need to focus on money, contacts, or credentials, as people want those who are highly engaged, rather than those trying simply to get by.

Remembering Forward—How It Works in the World: When was the last time you felt you made a positive contribution in your day? Did you step up and offer an insight at a meeting? Was it your participation in a volunteer activity? Perhaps it was a conversation with a friend in need. Whatever it was that made you feel as if you had a positive contribution, can you identify the characteristic that felt so good to you?

57

As you go through your day, remember forward with that feeling of positive contribution and resolve that you will contribute your best no matter the situation. The goal is to find the contribution you have to make and offer it each day. Even in small, subtle ways, it puts you on the path of expansion rather than having to stumble into random opportunities.

When you cease to make a contribution, you begin to die—
Eleanor Roosevelt

Mantra: *The world needs my unique contribution, and I offer it each day.*

Practice what if There is Nothing Wrong with You: As it is with so much of our natural beauty, the flame of our contribution is hidden under layers of doubt, denial and self-sabotage. You know what you have to offer the world. It may be something that will have a grand impact and mass appeal at some point. If you are ever going to arrive at your destiny, the journey must begin today. Begin practicing whatever contribution you long to make in the world; it is okay to start offering it now, however rough and "imperfect" it may be. There is nothing wrong with it or you, as you are the only one who can offer your gifts to the world. Those around you need it more than you know. Trust and take the next step.

From My Experience: Clients often come to me when there is a gap between what they know they can contribute and what they are offering in their day-to-day lives. They are "here" and want to get "there" and feel stymied by the inability to overcome perceived barriers like time, money, education and experience. The example I use is that someone wants to be a great chef, yet they don't feel that they can be one until they go to culinary school, have enough money for a professional kitchen and have cooked professionally for years. So instead, they plan to work in an office until they can achieve these benchmarks.

Stated this way, it seems preposterous; yet, that is how many people feel about making their contribution to the world. If you want to be a chef, starting cooking—cook anywhere you can, whenever you can. Enjoy it, share it, learn from it and grow into it. It is not only easier and fun this way; it is the only way to achieve it.

When I started my leadership work I had no idea I would be where I am now—and back then I wasn't capable of doing what I do now. Early presentations and lectures were highly scripted and, I am certain, not nearly as enjoyable. Today speaking one-on-one or to groups of thousands is thrilling as I am able to stand in the moment and speak from my heart. I couldn't do it in the same way all those years ago and if I had waited to become the speaker I am today before accepting those invitations, I would have never arrived here.

The way to making our contribution to the world is to start doing it now. The reward is not only your satisfaction, it is that you will change your world through your ever-increasing ability to give the best of yourself to others and the opportunities to do more of what you love will appear by your practicing making your contribution.

2nd Tuesday: Naming My Gifts

To give anything less than your best, is to sacrifice the gift —**Steve Prefontaine**

What Are My Unique Talents and Skills?

Early in the second week of our journey, we are continuing to make the abstract concrete. You know you have gifts and it is time to name them, to knowing who you truly are and to put concrete descriptors on these qualities. By naming your gifts, you not only create a solid foundation for your leadership journey, you allow others to access your talents easily. If you can't name it, no one else will be able to either. Conversely, by effectively communicating your talents to others, you allow people to easily connect to you and support your work in the world.

People's talents can be grouped into three overarching qualities. Write a list of all your talents, skills and strengths. Put as many items as you can on the list. Set the list aside for at least an hour and then return to it. Observe the similarities of various characteristics and put them into three groups. For instance, you may have "organized," "logical," and "detail-oriented" on your list, and perhaps the best way to encompass these qualities is that you are logistical, gifted in helping move projects through the various steps to completion. Whatever the three main characteristics you identify, they are the essential building blocks for your future work.

Remembering Forward—How It Works in the World: Have you ever noticed that people repeatedly compliment you on something you do? Do you throw great parties? Are you always organized for your meetings or have innovative solutions. Whatever it is that people often compliment you on, my guess is that you dismiss it because, "It is so easy, everyone can do it." Not true. It is easy for you because it is your gift and it isn't so easy for others, which is why they are complimenting you on it! Like other synchronicities in our life, attributes people vocalize about us are reflections of our talents we don't often see or acknowledge in ourselves.

In remembering forward today, reflect on the comments from others. What are they saying to you? How did it feel to be acknowledged for that quality? What did you do with it? Come up with a specific example of a time when you dismissed a compliment for something that now appears on your strengths and talents list; remember what it felt like to rebuff admiration. Now replay the scenario with you graciously accepting the praise and feel the difference. As you remember forward today, take that feeling of willingness to be seen for whom you are and the contribution you make to the world. For as you allow yourself to be seen, more and more will see you for who you truly are.

If we are to achieve a richer culture, rich in contrasting values, we must recognize the whole gamut of human potentialities, and so weave a less arbitrary social fabric, one in which each diverse human gift will find a fitting place—**Margaret Mead**

Mantra: *The three qualities that best define me are*

_____.

Practice What if There is Nothing Wrong With You: Once you have identified your three talents and strengths, the fun begins! Those qualities combined with your passion comprise the unique contribution you have to make in the world. As you stay present in practicing there is nothing wrong with you, begin to explore about what you are passionate. Because your passion and strengths are unique to you, not only is there nothing wrong with you, it is the gift the world has been waiting for you to express.

From My Experience: Very early in my career, I attended a time management seminar and subsequently was asked to give a presentation to the staff about what I had learned. I didn't think much about it and was surprised that nearly all of the 40-plus employees showed-up, including the firm's partners. I proceeded to give the hour-long talk and after returned to my office to tackle client challenges awaiting me.

Later, the vice president who asked me to give the presentation stopped by my office to thank me. In her comment's she said, "I don't know what you are going to do in your career and I'm sure it will include teaching. You did a fantastic job today." What? Huh? I was a political professional determined to help solve pressing public issues, I was NOT going to be a teacher.

Life has a funny way of providing us the opportunities to be at our best, even when we don't know it is happening. The comment has remained with me 22 years later and still makes me smile as speaking to groups is one of my greatest joys. Our natural talents shine through and when we are attune to what others reflect back to us, it gives us a chance to see what we may be missing and allow us to be more of who we already are.

2ⁿᵈ Wednesday: Complementary Qualities

True friendship can afford true knowledge. It does not depend on darkness and ignorance—**Henry David Thoreau**

What Qualities Do I Look For in Others?

As you become clear about your own unique talents and strengths, it opens you up to better understanding and appreciating those qualities in others. As the quote implies, the more truthful you are with yourself, the more confidently you can offer your truth to others, which allows them to do the same in return. And in this exchange lies a tremendous gift, that of appreciating complementary qualities in others and using them to enrich our lives.

Characteristics fall along various spectrums. For example, how we manage our time includes those on one end who are highly organized and exacting, and at the other end people who prefer to schedule and make decisions "when it feels right." Every quality is positive and one cannot possess traits at opposite ends of the spectrum, i.e., if you are highly organized and logical, being carefree and without plans is not a way of operating that will serve you best over the long term. When we embrace our talents, strengths and skills, we open to the possibilities of accepting others' and allowing their complementary attributes to enrich our lives. How wonderful to stop pressuring yourself to be more spontaneous if you are a planner and to allow those for whom it comes more naturally to guide you toward those moments when it can serve you, and others, well.

Remembering Forward—How It Works in the World: Can you remember a time when you looked at another person and were in awe of a talent or skill they possessed? The way he was able to do the right thing at the right moment, or perhaps the grace of another during a difficult conversation? Whether a trait or the skill of an artist or athlete, what you find alluring in others tells you much about yourself. Are you seeking those who are just like you, or those who share similar values and stretch you in other ways?

In remembering forward today, recall a time when it felt good to acknowledge the talent and skill of another and how that acknowledgement made you feel. Then look for the opportunity to remember forward and create that same circumstance today. Who in your world has a complementary skill? How does it feel to engage with that person based on your acknowledgement? And, how does that consciousness bring a new level of freedom and growth for both of you to move your relationship to a completely new level?

What we have done for ourselves alone dies with us; what we have done for others and the world remains immortal—**Albert Camus**

Mantra: *The three qualities that I look for in a relationship are*
_____.

Practice What if There is Nothing Wrong With You: In practicing what if there is nothing wrong with you, soon you come to a place where applying it to others is inevitable. The co-worker who is constantly correcting your typos, your sibling who never makes it anywhere on time or the partner who can't manage her finances — everyone in our life falls short of being the person we want them to be all the time. Ironically, the same holds true about you for them. If we come to the place of accepting that who we are is fine in this moment, then the opportunity to offer that same freedom to others is an amazing gift. In focusing on the qualities you admire in others and want in your relationships, you learn about yourself and are conscious and appreciative of those in your life.

From My Experience: I am a terrible speller. It has never come naturally to me as I recall hours spent memorizing spelling lists as a child. I felt defective during spelling bees and even as a professor sometimes stymied by something I wrote on the white board. I did everything I could to hide this deficiency from others.

In addition to being forever grateful for spellcheck (although sometimes I still get so stuck that I have to Google the word to even get me in the vicinity of the correct spelling!) my leadership journey has helped me to realize that it is okay to not be a great speller, it is because I have a systemic and strategic mind that focusing on details is more challenging for me. It has also freed me to appreciate the editors in my life, with their dreaded red pens, and to not feel bad about myself in the process of going back to correct the errors I've made. I value their contribution to ensuring what I write is correct and readable so that my ideas are written in a way that others can enjoy it.

This is just one example of how we tend to hide our "weaknesses," rather than to focus on our strengths and the strengths of others. Once we let go of the shame of not having a particular talent or strength we free ourselves, and others, to be at our best.

2nd Thursday: The Archetypes in Me

That which we do not bring to consciousness appears in our lives as fate—**Carl Jung**

What Are My Archetypes?

Archetypes are groups of qualities and characteristics inherited from our ancestors that are present in the collective unconscious and play out in our lives. The maiden, mother, the prodigal son, warrior and the wizard are all examples of archetypes deeply embedded in our psyche and on display regularly in our art, entertainment and lives. The gift of understanding archetypes, like all other leadership characteristics, is in examining our behavioral patterns through a different lens. We appreciate how to free ourselves from unintended consequences of these patterns and to embrace fully the positive traits at work in us daily.

Joseph Campbell, Caroline Myss and, of course, Carl Jung have written extensively on archetypes, and there are numerous others who have explored archetypal behavior throughout history to current day. Discovering your archetypes will guide you through a process of examining them at work in your life, and you will soon see them appear everywhere—with colleagues, friends, family and in entertainment. You will never watch another movie without seeing them play out in vivid color while providing a venue to learn how they act and interact with one another. Harness the power of archetypes and watch how you're understanding of yourself and group dynamics begins to open up to greater understanding—insights that allow you bridge differences and move forward in life with grace.

Remembering Forward—How It Works in the World: Take a few quiet moments to close your eyes and relax. Allow your mind to go back to the books, movies and stories that have had the greatest impact on you. With which characters do you most relate? Why? What are the qualities that those characters possess that resonate with you? Move through the stories and characters until you have discerned a pattern. As soon as you open your eyes, write down the characters and characteristics. Keep in mind some of those with whom you have identified may be animals, fantasy characters or other fictional beings. All characters are helpful as each allows you to better understand yourself, i.e., the lone wolf, diva or space warrior. You can repeat this exercise and look for the archetypes of people that are frequently in your life. Do you often find yourself with the rebel or the intellectual? Why is that? And is it serving you well?

As you remember forward today, bring these archetypical patterns alive in you. Where there may be wisps or shades in your life make them Technicolor. Bring these archetypes alive in your interactions, meetings and casual exchanges and observe how differently you feel. Also, note the shift in how others respond to you and your brighter archetypal qualities along with the newfound power and clarity in your communications.

Today marks the moment when the reflection of the past 11 days begins to transform the person you are in the world. Let your colors shine brightly in the understanding that who you are is rooted in the vast archetypal experience we share as humans. You are a unique expression of qualities we share and today, and everyday hereafter, is an opportunity to let them shine brightly.

The only person you are destined to become is the person you decide to be—**Ralph Waldo Emerson**

Mantra: *I am the _____ archetype, and its positive qualities are apparent in me today.*

Practice What if There is Nothing Wrong With You: As with all qualities we exhibit, archetypes have their shadow along with light. Can you allow yourself to be with both sides of your archetype without judgment? Has the rebel been belligerent simply for the sake of rebelling "without a cause?" Has the mother given without allowing herself to receive? Has the hero become addicted to the adulation? Without making yourself, or others, wrong, can you accept the spectrum of behavior and allow yourself consciously to choose differently? The next time you feel the rebel, mother or hero emerge, allow yourself to move toward the positive qualities expressed by your archetypes and allow those qualities in the shadow to dissipate. The shadow teaches us to appreciate the light, feel gratitude and move toward becoming the best of who you already are.

From My Experience: Until now, I have introduced the concept of working with one's archetypes only with the clients who have done intensive retreats with me as the process I use takes a few hours and necessitates quiet reflection afterward. Interestingly, those who have identified their archetypes and where they are at play in their lives, find it to be one of the most useful tools to guide their leadership day-to-day. The exercise I've created for this book is a good start and one that will open the door to greater exploration because archetypes are a powerful key to our calling and conduct.

For me, the discovery of the Guide as a key archetype put many parts of my work into a fresh and liberating perspective. A guide is someone who is on the journey with you, who walks a few steps ahead and supports you taking the best steps while avoiding potential hazards and pitfalls. A guide faces the unknown, willing to learn and to share their knowledge with those who are on or will walk the path.

In engaging with my archetypes, I discovered why coach, teacher and even professor had never felt quite right as these people stand apart and tell others what to do. A guide, like the leader I discuss, walks with those he or she serves—and that is who I am. In discovering the Guide as one of my archetypes, it unleashed greater clarity about my work—including the guidebook, you are currently reading! Aware of them or not, our archetypes are at work within us and when we cooperate with them they will show us wonderful ways to put our leadership into the world.

2nd Friday: How Am I in Relationships?

To be fully seen by somebody...and loved anyhow, this is a human offering that can border on the miraculous—**Elizabeth Gilbert**

What Are the Best Qualities I Express in Relationships?

Leadership is relationship; being a leader implies that you have decided to consciously engage in relationships. Making conscious choices is one of the three pillars of leadership skills (effective communication and using conflict as tools for growth are the other two). Therefore, leading in relationships starts not with the other; it begins with you. How are you showing up in the relationships in your life?

In working with hundreds of clients, most come to the leadership development process motivated by relationships that are not working: a boss or co-workers, family or friends, even intimates and neighbors; whoever it is, people feeling that others are standing in the way of them doing what they want. However frustrating another's behavior may be, the place to begin changing the dynamics starts within because what is going on in relationships with others is a reflection of what is happening within us. We are bothered first by the inconsistencies in our alignment; that is, who we are, what we want and what we are saying are not in sync, so we are not fully and harmoniously connecting with others, resulting in unsatisfying and unhappy relationships.

Once we become clear that being our best in relationships and speaking our truth is the *only* way forward, we find that the expression of our leadership is not a deterrent to harmony with others, it is the foundation of gratifying relationships. Expressing ourselves is not the cause of conflict; how others choose to respond to our needs, feelings and desires is at the root of the issues. The only way to move forward is to be clear and provide the opportunity for others to do so as well. Keeping ourselves hidden may feel safe, and only in being fully seen can we open the door to connection and ultimate love. It is the same love that animates action—in other words, leadership.

Remembering Forward—How It Works in the World

In talking with groups about how best to present themselves in the world, I suggest that success in public speaking comes from being comfortable being "naked" in front of others. This is, of course, metaphoric, and today's remembering forward comes by recalling a time when you allowed yourself to be "naked" with others. What did you let go of, to drop your barriers and fully show up as you? How did the others respond? My guess is that you found new levels of connection and peace by leading with your true self, and you cleared the way for those around you to do the same. Identify that feeling and use it to be fully yourself in all relationships today. At the end of the day, observe how your leadership enhanced these interactions.

No one can make you feel inferior without your consent—**Eleanor Roosevelt**

Mantra: *Being my best in relationships is the way to improve all my relationships.*

Practice What if There is Nothing Wrong With You: Many people hide in relationships because they believe there is something wrong with them. How can I express what I am feeling? Or what I need? Even what I desire, if I believe that somehow I don't deserve to get what I want? We cannot be met in life if we don't show up and ask others for what we want. Today, practice that there is nothing wrong with you by leading in your relationships. Be open, honest, sincere and *direct* about what is important to you and then allow others to respond. Remember your job is to be the best of you, and what others chose to do is a reflection of them not you.

From My Experience: Nothing trips people up more than the idea that one must be honest about what they are experiencing with the people they care about. How can I tell my boss, partner

74

or friend I'm unhappy with something? It seems evident that problems cannot be addressed if they can't be acknowledged and discussed and yet it is how most people approach others in the lives.

I've learned, actually, I'm probably still learning, that nothing good comes out of denying my feelings. My feelings are real and right, wrong, good or bad, they are mine—and my feelings directly impact how I show-up in relationships. If I am not feeling good about something, I can't be fully engaged and effective when dealing with that person.

I've come to practice a two-fold process when dealing with expressing myself in relationships. One is to look at what is bothering me and to examine where the root of the issue exists within me; that is, if I don't feel that someone is paying enough attention to my needs, where am I ignoring myself? Or perhaps the needs of the other person? Two, in discussing my feeling with others, I own my responsibility for my experience and I don't blame the other for causing me to feel a certain way. By staying in my power to create my experience, I lead in the discussion by taking blame out of the equation and allow for open sharing. When I add clarity about my needs, wants and desires I've created a path to move beyond the issue before us and onto a stronger and healthier relationship.

2nd Saturday: What Is My Purpose in Life?

The purpose of life is a life of purpose—**Robert Byrne?**

What is the Purpose In What I Do?

Everyone has that moment when he or she stops and wonders, "What the heck am I doing here?" Be it in the middle of a hectic day or in an infrequent moment when peace and calm finally descend—the question seeks to connect us to the larger purpose of our life, not the daily monotony that easily takes over our lives. Whatever the impetus, the questioning awakens you to the awareness that you once had dreams, that you were inspired by your passion and that you came here to contribute something important to the world. The challenge for many is that they believe they don't know what that purpose is or what they "should" be doing. In remaining stuck and adrift, it is easier to wander through life than taking responsibility for what is happening or not.

For those that take action toward the desire for something more, the answer is at hand. One's purpose is found in bringing forth their unique set of talents and strengths to create the change they want to see in the world. In addition to reading this book and working through the exercises, begin reflecting on what you would like to be different in the world. Whatever it is that you want to be different; it is the gateway to your purpose. Now is the time to walk through the door.

Remembering Forward—How It Works in the World: Reflect back on your early childhood as you did last week. What did you want to be when you grew up? A firefighter? Doctor? Astronaut? While these answers are not necessarily the careers you are destined for, they are archetypes that reveal clues to your purpose. Did you want to be the firefighter who saved people? Or was it his bravery in the face of danger? Was being a doctor about caring for the sick or finding a cure for a disease?

In remembering forward today, reach back to that child who dreamed that anything was possible. What did you want to contribute to the world?

Write down the answer to that question and then live it today. Do at least one thing that brings the essence of that desired change into your life. And if you keep doing this every day, within a few short weeks you will *know* your purpose and will have already begun living it.

The mystery of human existence lies not in just staying alive, but in finding something to live for—**Fyodor Dostoyevsky,** ***The Brothers Karamazov***

Mantra: *My purpose lives in the change I wish to bring into the world.*

Practice What if There is Nothing Wrong with You: One of the first, and most insidious, splits in our lives begins when we start believing that who we are isn't good enough. Our dreams of being a dancer, teacher or President are squashed knowingly and not by adults who convey what was once taught to them: that you can't be yourself and thrive in the world. As children, you adapt to this message by either throwing your dreams aside or overcommitting yourself to your vision at the cost of all else in your life. Today, give yourself the gift of reconnecting with the child in you who still believes that you can do what you love and be successful in life. Once you find that part of you, reflect on how your life would be different today if you had always lived as if you could be, do and have all you desire. When you arrive in the present moment, do something real and tangible now that solidifies the belief that you can be what you dreamed of, so long ago. For example, engage with your co-workers as if you always were enthusiastic and confident, or take a walk with the curiosity and wonder of discovering something new. Life viewed from the vantage point of your "untainted" self, without the limiting beliefs instilled by you and others, takes on expanded possibilities and is much more fun. Enjoy living your purpose, and mindfully bring it forward from now on.

From My Experience: Returning to our childhood dreams is an exercise that has many benefits. Last week we used it to connect to passion and today we use it to seek insights into our purpose. Both are inextricably linked and powerful tools to unleash your leadership.

When I was five-years-old, I wanted to be the first woman President of the United States—I longed to solve problems and make the world a better place. That desire propelled me into activities and study aimed at becoming an elected official. Like other young people, as I moved through early adulthood I was living my dream without understanding my purpose. My purpose is to guide individuals to lead, to be at their best and contribute it to our communities so that we address the challenges facing us.

Being President isn't the best way to live my purpose, although at some point it could be an option. If I had focused my career on becoming President, I would have missed years of practicing, doing and living what I am best at. Even more poignantly, if I were to have become President, I wouldn't have been able to serve and lead the way that I longed to as a child because my entire life would have consisted of pursuits and activities that were not in alignment with my passion and purpose.

While often asked, I do not know if running for elected office is in my future or not. What I know is that whatever I chose to do, it will be something I passionately pursue that allows me to guide people to lead and create solutions. If becoming President allows me the opportunity to do that in the best possible way, great—and if not, then I will be happily living my purpose in some other way. And a life of happiness was ultimately the dream of that little girl.

2nd Sunday: When Am I At My Best?

There is no passion to be found playing small—in settling for a life that is less than the one you are capable of living—**Nelson Mandela**

How Do I Feel When I am Having a Peak Experience?

The moments in your life when you experience pure joy and connection are peak experiences. Some people find them when engaged in athletics, others in meditation or simply by being in nature. Where or how you reach that moment is less important than the fact that you allow yourself to taste this life truth—who you are in this moment is perfect, and experiencing this allows you to feel good. Often people believe that peak experiences must be achieved in an act of doing something extraordinary, rather than understanding that they are found in the simplicity of being you. Activities allow you to distract your mind with something you enjoy so that your full self comes forward. If you allow yourself to be fully present more often, you will enjoy more frequent and greater peak experiences.

The beauty of a peak experience and the insights leading up to it are guideposts to exercising your leadership. As you allow yourself to get lost in activities and enjoy them with your body, mind and soul, you are fully engaged on all levels. When was the last time you had a peak experience? What did it feel like? What caused that moment of perfection to arise? Today we are exploring this high as a way to understand not how far you have to go, rather to begin contemplating how close you are to what you desire.

Remembering Forward—How it Works in the World: As you review your peak experiences, reflect on how you experienced what was real and present in that moment. So much of what we experience in our daily lives is the *worst* of our past, rather than the best. This is a vital part of the remembering forward concept—we can choose to remember the best of our lives and

81

not the worst. In the coming days, I will introduce tools to help you release past memories so that they don't set the narrative now or in the future. For today, practice bringing the best forward. Relive one peak experience in your life, and bring forward that moment of transcendence to see how your experience today *and* tomorrow shift.

The person in peak-experiences feels himself, more than other times, to be the responsible, active, creating center of his activities and of his perceptions. He feels more like a prime-mover, more self-determined (rather than caused, determined, helpless, dependent, passive, weak, bossed). He feels himself to be his own boss, fully responsible, fully volitional, with more "free-will" than at other times, master of his fate, an agent—**Abraham Maslow**

Mantra: *My peak experiences create future experiences.*

Practice What if There is Nothing Wrong With You: There is nothing wrong with having a peak experience and then returning to "real life." We must have the lows to appreciate the highs, and by being aware of the peaks and valleys, we can use this practice to move to greater heights and less dramatic lows. By not "cursing the darkness" or lows, you can bring yourself to a neutral place—i.e., not experiencing great highs or lows. Release the thoughts that something is wrong and focus on the expansiveness found in peak experiences. Most people believe that peak experiences are intended to be few and far between rather that the places from which to set the standard of the new normal. There is nothing wrong with you. Align with your peak experiences, and allow yourself to reach new heights and open up your life to the peaks you cannot see from your vantage point today.

From My Experience: It is amazing to me how many people believe that peak experiences are to be the exception rather than the rule. I see it at play with clients who believe that if they allow their full power to come forward then what will be left for them to desire. If I am leading at my best, out on the leading edge and achieving all I desire, how will I go on if I have everything I want?

Herein lies the trap—if we achieve what we want and desire then there will be nothing left to want and desire, so I won't allow myself to have it all, so that there is always something more to want and desire. An endless cycle that keeps us from experiencing all we can because we fail to understand this: every time you reach a peak, the next one becomes clear and only becomes clear from that new vantage point.

How often I find myself in this vicious cycle working toward manifesting a goal and yet a part of me not wanting it to happen for fear I won't have any motivation. I've described the feeling like driving a car with one foot on the gas pedal and one on the break. You don't get very far and you spend a lot of energy getting there!

When I began allowing more frequent peak experiences into my life, I found the joy and satisfaction they brought felt wonderful and catalyzed the realization of exploring many new frontiers. I never thought I would write anything people wanted to read. When I got positive feedback on handouts and exercises from groups, it led me to blogging, from there the idea of writing a book came and so on to the point that I am now excited about adding several more books to this series and I've started writing a screenplay!

Without the courage to enjoy the fruits of our leadership, we hem ourselves in from all that we can be. Peak experiences are fun and more of them are even better.

3rd Monday: How Do I Offer My Gifts, Receive From Others and Cultivate Love?

Until we can receive with an open heart, we're never really giving with an open heart. When we attach judgment to receiving help, we knowingly or unknowingly attach judgment to giving help— **Brené Brown**

How Am I Giving and Receiving?

As we begin the second half of the 28-day course, we shift our focus to taking our leadership into the world. While leadership begins within, what is showing up in our life is the biggest indicator of what's working and what isn't. The next two weeks focus on walking our love in the world—that is, our leadership.

Nothing creates more anxiety in leaders than the idea of giving and receiving. In the traditional model of leadership, the "giving", i.e., orders, directions, etc., is done by the leader who is then "served" by subordinates. In healthy relationships of all kind, giving and receiving are done with *equality.* This does not mean quid pro quo, where each person does the exact same things for the other. On the contrary, it is the recognition of the unique talents and strengths of individuals and allowing each person to give *and* receive in equal measure. The key is that each person's needs are met by the strengths of the other at the right moment. In order to give in this way, you must be willing to acknowledge and articulate what you need and to allow others to bring their leadership to you at the right time and in the right way.

Remembering Forward—How It Works in the World:
Remembering times when you were giving the best of yourself to a person or group is, often, an easy task. Allow yourself to identify at least three times in your life when you felt "in service" to others that required the best of what you have to offer the world. Next, reflect on those moments when you allowed someone to do the same for you, identifying the situation when

you were "in need." It is easier to think of feeling great about helping a homeless person find a meal and shelter, rather than to recognize the time when you were in desperate need of a meal just under different circumstances. Did you receive with the same grace in which you gave?

In remembering forward today, feel into the space of receiving and *ask* someone for something you need today—and then go give that very same thing to someone else—as best as you can. If you want more humor and joy in your life first ask your friend or partner to participate in an opportunity to laugh and then go provide it for someone else in whatever way you can. The world is created through this dynamic: if you give what you are asking for, you will experience a shift in your perspective that allows you to receive it. For example, if you want more money in your life, give money to someone, through an extra tip, a friend in need, whatever situation presents itself to you. It need not be in the same quantity you desire, and you will see a dynamic develop that opens up possibilities for you and others. Trust me—you are in for a huge surprise, and make sure to write your experience in your journal.

Trying to get without first giving is as fruitless as trying to reap without having sown—**Napoleon Hill**

Mantra: *I give what I wish to receive; I receive and give with grace.*

Practice What if There is Nothing Wrong With You: When you believe that something is wrong with you, a barrier to the outside world is created. While you feel the wall protects you from being seen, you fail to understand it also keeps you from receiving what you truly desire. Yes, we may be able to lob our gifts over the wall and into the world, yet it is a terribly inefficient way for you to live; the flow and dynamic engagement with the world is suppressed, diminishing your light, impact and happiness. As you feel into the notion that there is nothing wrong with you today, become aware of the "barrier" that "protects" you in and from the world. As you go through your day, notice when you're giving and receiving are hindered by this wall, and then consciously lower it *in the moment.* Observe how the dynamic changes in that situation, and how much more you and the others around you are able to experience as a result of just you shifting. This is change; this is leadership—as you shift, so does everything around you.

From My Experience: For those who pride themselves on helping others—this can be a tough concept. Many of us who grew up without our fundamental needs being met allowed our coping mechanism to became doing for others what wasn't being done for us. While the concept is noble, it is a flawed practice and creates harm as people find themselves in a loop of giving more and more of what they desire to fill a hole of what they are unable to allow themselves to receive.

The times I built strong connections were in symbiotic relationships—ones in which we were both giving and receiving. People use their talents to "help" us all the time: doctors, chefs, merchants—they provide a service and we pay them, a straightforward give and take. This becomes more challenging in organizations when asking a colleague for technical insights for a report might be construed as a weakness. After all, why can't you do the report on your own?

Yet, we feel no shame in asking a chef to prepare a meal for us that we couldn't prepare ourselves; and it is a wonderful opportunity to be grateful for another's talents even beyond the compensation given to him. When I acknowledge to others that they have talents I don't possess we both feel better. Moreover, it lowers my resistance to actually getting what I want because I often don't enjoy doing the things others do so well.

Some of the most rewarding professional relationships I've developed are with those who provide complimentary services to what I offer. By acknowledging where their talents are helpful and beyond my scope, it allows me to receive what they have to offer and brings richness to my life and work. It doesn't mean that what I do isn't special, important or limited. It means that we recognize the dedication each has had to their work and instead of competing with one another, we bolster each other. As a result, we often end up sharing clients as they can benefit from the complimentary gifts as well -- a win for everyone!

3rd Tuesday: How Do I Make Choices?

Every man builds his world in his own image. He has the power to choose, but no power to escape the necessity of choice—**Ayn Rand**

Am I Aware of the Choices I Make?

Regardless if you want to accept it or not, *everything* you do is choice. Getting out of bed, going to a job, who you associate with, where you live, everything is a choice. Most people would say many aspects of their life are chosen for them, i.e., "I need a job for money so I can eat," "This house is all I can afford," "I can't move out of the community," etc. Except the reality is that when you do not make a choice, you are, by default, choosing that option. Understanding that you are making choices in every circumstance is a cornerstone of effective leadership, because once you grasp that you are driving the car and not the other way around, you become empowered to choose what you want in your life.

One of the best ways to understand the power of choice is to use your body as a way of understanding choices you are making in the moment. When you get up in the morning, how are you feeling? Are you overwhelmed by the day ahead, or do you feel good and empowered around the way in which you are choosing to begin your day? The way you feel is an excellent measure of the choices you are making and your awareness around those choices. When you are making choices in your best interest, the body responds with lightness and good health. Even if the job you went to this morning isn't your dream job, you *are* choosing it in this moment because it offers you a paycheck. If you can harness the power of the choice you are making and the control you have over that choice, you will be on a path toward greater clarity. At first, this clarity may only come in the form of a shift in perspective, and soon it will manifest itself in exercising the power you have to choose differently to create different outcomes.

Remembering Forward—How It Works in the World: Remember a moment when you made a split-second decision, a time when "thinking" was not an option and a choice had to be made—now. Perhaps you swerved your car to avoid an accident, or maybe you told someone you loved him or her even though you hadn't planned to say anything. Moments of urgency offer us the opportunity to make choices without contemplation and experience the deliciousness of choice without thought. In these moments, our true self comes forward. Most often, undesired outcomes are the result of fearing being yourself and it gets in the way of clear choice. Conversely, when you are "forced" to choose an option that may scare you, often that one leads you along your true path, as you don't have time to think yourself out of it. Today, remember forward by creating those moments of euphoria when the choice of your true self became evident, and look for a moment when you can make a similar choice— without needing the sense of urgency to cause you to do so.

There are no safe choices. Only other choices—**Libba Bray, *A Great and Terrible Beauty***

Mantra: *I choose and in that choice, I create my life.*

Practice what if there is nothing wrong with you: True choice is the living embodiment of the belief that there is nothing wrong with you, because conscious choice by its own nature must come from a place of wholeness. Only by believing that there is nothing wrong with you can you come to know that choices rooted in the truth of who you are will create the best outcomes. As you move through your day, pause before each choice, root yourself in the belief that there is nothing wrong with you, and then choose. Observe the different outcomes you experience as a result and record them in your journal.

From My Experience: Head, heart and gut are the three places that people refer to when making choices. More often than not, people single out one of these filters as the default for choice making. Alternatively, they may rely on one in certain situations and another in others. Moments of true clarity are when the three are aligned and the choice natural.

I've developed my choice muscle by observing where in my body I'm making my decisions. If you haven't figured out by this point, my strong intellect and intuition meant I often relied on those qualities to guide me forward. As I've matured, I realized that without the heart and reverence for my feelings as an equal component to what's right for the situation and the other, my choices often didn't result in my happiness.

My professional life had been built around Washington, D.C. for most of my career. When my life there was no longer flowing the way it once did, I kept intellectualizing why I should stay to avoid making new choices. Finally, one cold day sitting in the car in my driveway, I understood it was time for me to move—my heart understood what my head and gut had been trying to say finally. I longed for experiences in my life that could not be found inside the Beltway. Once head, heart and gut were aligned, the choice was obvious—and remarkably easy.

In going against what I was experiencing on all levels and trying to rationalize against choosing change, I was limiting myself. Once I listened to all of me and made the choice to move to the West Coast, so many options open in my life. Ironically, one of the greatest was the opportunity to transform the systems in DC, which is much easier when you are not a part of them day-to-day—and what I've always longed to do.

Choice is the fabric of our lives and it regularly scares us. Once we make choice a leadership tool we grab hold of our lives and our power. Choosing to lead becomes a way of life and not an occasional activity and that is how you change your reality and the world.

3rd Wednesday: How Do I Practice Acceptance? Responsibility?

Remember always that you not only have the right to be an individual you have an obligation to be one—**Eleanor Roosevelt**

How Do I Accept Responsibility for Me?

What if, your greatest responsibility in life was to be your best? That is it; nothing more is required of you other than to be your best throughout your entire life. It is eloquently simple and challenging beyond imagination. Our best often feels difficult. You don't want to give 100 percent to the report that's due or to the client who will never know if you cut a few corners, or the patient, student or child that doesn't need your full attention for you to "get by." You know you aren't always at your best, but does it really matter?

The challenge is that too often we equate being our best with being perfect. Nothing is less synonymous. Being your best means showing up fully in the moment, giving the best of what you have and being honest about what that is in the moment. In that honesty, you are at your best. The surest way consistently to offer your best is to be fully aware and focused on the now and to take full responsibility for sharing what you can offer in the immediate situation. Your best changes as you do. By acknowledging what your best is in the moment everyone is clear about the contribution being made and the best outcomes are reached. For example, you can communicate with your supervisor that a report completed in one day, will not be as good as if you can have the three days it will take to do your best. You lead from a position of clarity that allows others to decide what is best for them given the circumstances and you are both enable each other's leadership.

Just as important is to reflect on how you show up for you. Do you practice your best for yourself, physically, mentally, emotionally and spiritually? Being responsible for yourself begins with self-care, and the action comes from taking responsibility for you in every moment—what is showing up in your life is a reflection of how you think and feel about yourself. By mindfully accepting responsibility for you and your life, you can be your best as you move through whatever occurs in your day.

Remembering Forward—How It Works in the World: In accepting responsibility for yourself, consider that acceptance removes the judgment around your thoughts. Responsibility means you have the ability to choose how you "respond" to what is present. When judgment recedes, true responsibility emerges because we become aware of what truly is—not what was experienced through a judgmental lens. Today we strip remembering forward to its core—to its presence in your life, whether you are aware of it or not. Remembering forward is how we live as our past experiences are ever informing our present ones. The responsibility you have is to choose between remembering forward from your pain or your love. Begin to weave this concept with what if nothing is wrong with you to begin to see, feel and live your past without the (mis)judgments of pain that create what you don't want in your future. Today become aware of how you're remembering makes you feel in this moment and choose responsibly how you bring those emotions forward or not.

God, grant me the serenity to accept the things I cannot change. The courage to change the things I can. And the wisdom to know the difference—**Reinhold Niebuhr**

Mantra: *In this moment, all is perfect—and I accept responsibility for any thought that tells me otherwise.*

Practice What if There is Nothing Wrong With You: Our past experiences are continually shaping our present. The problem with past experiences being a guidepost to today is that they make tomorrow exactly, or nearly, the same. Issues linger because the beliefs that created them don't change reality. Today, see what IS in your life as perfect for what it is today. No judgments, no fears, no anxiety—just be okay with what is, because that is the best ground to take responsibility for the next step in your life.

From My Experience: The toughest and most powerful work I've done with myself relates to today's lesson and the power to take responsibility for my life based on the now rather than the past. I experienced a great deal of trauma as a child. The way I survived was by making certain pronouncements about who I was. For example, the impossible want for a happy home and healthy family as a child became internalized as, "I don't get what I want," and further, although I don't "I'm going to be successful anyway."

On the plus side, the drive and determination to succeed helped me to achieve a great deal well beyond my years; unfortunately, the belief that I don't get what I want was still playing out in my life and kept true happiness at bay for years longer than I would have liked. A child in pain created these beliefs and yet without consciousness around them they were running my life. What took years to understand is that I wasn't an innocent bystander, I was a co-conspirator as I was choosing, unconsciously, or not, to continue to allow them the run my life.

When I finally got to a point where I wanted to get what I wanted in my life, I had to take responsibility for why it wasn't showing up—and the only place to look was in the mirror. While there is often sadness for years of allowing the patterns to play out, continuing the misery is not the point of the exercise, responsibility and choice are.

When I chose to let the choices of a small, scared girl go and to begin taking responsibility for my thoughts, actions and deeds each day, things changed. They shifted as I was able to start seeing all the times I did get what I wanted, how strong I was in standing up for others in getting what they truly desired and how acknowledging that I too could, and often did, have what I

95

desired brought more of what I wanted into my life. When I understood that what was happening in my life was not a mystery, but rather the result of my choices, and then I had the opportunity to make new choices. Once I started doing that, my world changed and continues to change every day.

3rd Thursday: How Do I Balance Desire with the Present Moment?

Men go too far greater lengths to avoid what they fear than to obtain what they desire—**Dan Brown,** ***The Da Vinci Code***

How Can Desire Lead Me Forward, Not Pull on My Past?

Fear lives in the past, and desire that grows out of past fears does not allow the creation of a different future. Feeling as if you never have enough money only creates more of the same, no matter how much you wish to create more wealth. The only way to allow desires to become reality is to allow them to emanate from the present—a perfect present free of the fears, anxiety and disapproval that reside in your head, not in truth.

Everyone wants to have happiness, love and abundance in their life. Too often people look for things in their life to be the source of those feelings, i.e., do I have money, good relationships and fun times? If those qualities or experiences are absent, people often try to change the external realities by getting a better job, finding a different relationship or group of friends. The truth is that nothing outside of you will create what you desire until you are able to reach those states of well-being even in the absence of the physical expression. The goal is not to make your world as you want it and *then* to be happy; rather, it is knowing that it is our being peaceful in the moment that makes it so in the world. Leaders understand their ability to have an impact emanates from their grace in the moment and from the desires that are manifested from a peaceful now rather than a fearful past.

Remembering Forward—How It Works in the World:

Remembering forward is a great asset when we find the good feelings we *know* happened and use them to create a desirable future. In the same way, most of us are using past negative experiences to create a future that isn't what we want. The lesson today is to truly become aware of this phenomenon and consciously use it to create. What is real in the present? What is possible in the future? Moreover, why does your past so often control from a negative memory rather than a positive one? Today and each day ahead, let go of negative experiences that keep you believing you can't have or be what you desire. From the present moment, all things are possible—as long as you allow yourself to be open to the possibility; you can create what you desire in the next moment.

I've come to know that what we want in life is the greatest indication of who we really are—**Richard Paul Evans**

Mantra: *I choose in the present moment to see my desires becoming reality.*

Practice What if There is Nothing Wrong with You: The reason that so many people believe that nothing is going to change in the future or that there is something wrong in the present is because they believe that the past has made them unworthy of their dreamed future. What if nothing is wrong with you? If there is truly nothing wrong with you, then why can't you create what you desire in your life? If we allow ourselves to release our past conditioning that tells us "we already know" what the future holds based on past experience, we allow ourselves, and most importantly others, to show up differently in the NOW. That is how the future changes. Not by happenstance, rather by showing up in the present and making choices that lead to the future you desire.

From My Experience: Unsurprisingly, while writing this chapter, I am faced with a situation that goes to the heart of this lesson; a reminder that when we shift our leadership, the world provides us the opportunity to put it into practice. Living the leadership choice means that as events swirl we have the opportunity to meet them from an expanded perspective rather than relying on our conditioned norms.

Whenever I am faced with a situation that creates strong desire in me that is different from the current situation, I understand my choices are two-fold. First, I must accept responsibility for creating the situation and in accepting responsibility, I take back my power. By seeing that the "issue" before me was created when I stepped out of my power I also have the opportunity to rectify the thinking that caused me to feel powerless. Simply, if I am the reason the situation exists then I hold the key to solving it—and in that awareness, I can.

Second, I must look for the good in the now as the basis to moving forward. When I focus on the good that has come out of situation, I relinquish the self-flagellation and can be grateful that, at a minimum, I've understood what didn't work and am addressing it so that it won't happen again. I can't go back and change the past and by shifting my attitude to being glad for the lesson and wisdom, I more easily move through difficulties.

I understand what I've said isn't easy to do. We don't like what someone has done or are angry about how we were treated—it is natural to feel hurt, angry and want to lash out. When you are facing an intensely emotional experience, allow yourself to feel the emotions and use this as a time to reflect rather than react. Once you have released the initial feelings it is easier to find the pain in the situation—yours and theirs. The pain was created the moment *you* stepped away from your leadership and can't be changed; and now you have a choice to move forward with a different perspective.

In this moment, your desire is to feel better, to find happiness, joy, success, etc. And the only way it becomes possible is to begin creating anew from the now. What is real for you and how can you use the now to move you forward? The balance is found in reclaiming your power and resolving mindfully to act in this moment and to do so with great clarity and alignment.

3rd Friday: How Do I Detach From Outcomes and Accept Uncertainty?

I wanted a perfect ending. Now I've learned, the hard way, that some poems don't rhyme, and some stories don't have a clear beginning, middle, and end. Life is about not knowing, having to change, taking the moment and making the best of it, without knowing what's going to happen next. Delicious Ambiguity—
Gilda Radner

How Do I Trust That What is Coming is Better Than I Can Imagine?

The great paradox of creating, manifesting or realizing our dreams is that it easily happens when you let go of how it looks—which is exactly the opposite of how we are told to create it. While visioning, picturing and imagining are parts of the process, the key is to focus on how you feel having it. To achieve your goals, picture them even greater than you can imagine and then focus the experience of living it. Don't be a bystander or an audience watching it; live it from the inside out, put yourself on the court, stage, podium—wherever you dream to be and then let go of the image and keep the feeling with you.

What happens after engaging with the image of our desire, our past creeps forward to try to tell you *how* your desire is going to manifest—and then all is lost. Because once we shift to the dreaded "how," our brilliant minds tell us that what we envision is implausible. "Is my boss really going to promote me and give me a raise?" Maybe, and if that is the job and salary you want, is there a possibility that someone might leave and you would be promoted, or that a new position might open up? There are infinite possibilities that could allow your desires to manifest. Without being conscious of your mental chatter, your rational mind tells you the chances are nearly impossible. Accepting the uncertainty means that you trust in infinite possibilities, and in trusting the ambiguity, you allow your desires to come to fruition quickly and easily.

Remembering Forward—How It Works in the World: In remembering forward today, reflect on a time when something that you truly desired just "showed up" in your life. Did you run into a former classmate, who led you to a perfect job? Was there a call from a friend that kept you from disaster? Or perhaps it was an offer you could never have imagined that changed the course of your life? Find at least one example of this type of occurrence in your life, and then think about what you were wanting just before it happened. Did you want more adventure in your life? Did you want an opportunity to put your talents into the world in a different way? Were you hoping for more peace? Whatever it was, feel into that moment and keep the feeling going to when you received it. My guess is that it felt like magic.

Leaders understand how to harness the power of drawing to them what they desire by knowing that they are leading in their lives. Remember forward today by bringing that feeling to something you wish to create now—and see how it shows up in your life.

*Let go of certainty. The opposite isn't uncertainty. It's openness, curiosity and a willingness to embrace paradox, rather than choose up sides. The ultimate challenge is to accept ourselves exactly as we are, but never stop trying to learn and grow—***Tony Shwartz**

Mantra: *I choose my future by allowing it to manifest in unimaginable ways.*

Practice What if There is Nothing Wrong With You: By now, you are experiencing the power of releasing negative self-perceptions that keep you from being fully present and interfering with your desired future. It is the belief that there is something wrong with you that keeps you from trusting the future. Because, if your only frame of reference is that you are somehow less than perfect, then how can what you want ever come to you? If there is nothing wrong with you, then it is a simple step to your desires; no barriers, no twisting, no becoming something different, just being okay with who and where you are now and knowing that what comes will meet you in your wholeness.

From My Experience: Riding the wave of change and uncertainty is at the core of our journey and this experience only feels good when we feel good about ourselves. We know that we have the choice to view the glass as half-empty or half-full and are we able to meet life experiences from the viewpoint that we are getting the glass we've been asking for.

When positive change occurs, we see it as evidence that got what we wanted. Likewise, when the unexpected shows-up, do we want what we got? Through the leadership lens, we can see how what is showing up is what we want, even if it doesn't look like we thought it would; and if we can view it from this perspective it will become an opportunity and not a challenge.

In my life, and with my clients, I see this phenomenon all the time. People want a shift in careers and then a new board is elected and—poof, they have three months to find a new job. Or perhaps they have wanted more time to spend on a creative project and—bang, a health issue comes up that keeps them at home for a month. In these, and countless other examples like them, there is a choice. The choice to see how you got what you wanted or to lament a tragedy that occurred, and one way or another, you will have to move forward from the present. If you can find the gift of getting what you wanted in everything, you will have a much easier time moving toward what you desire from a leadership mindset.

3rd Saturday: How Do I Serve in the World?

How wonderful it is that nobody need wait a single moment before starting to improve the world—**Anne Frank**

How Do My Actions Impact the World?

Ask the majority of people, and they have great aspirations for the world—peace, prosperity, and happiness for all. In the most abstract terms, you wish for others what you wish for yourself. Yet, when those same people are asked how they are creating peace, prosperity and happiness in their lives for themselves and others, they come to an abrupt halt. How can I possibly do all that? I have a job, bills, kids, etc. All those things keep you from having the capacity to add world peace to your plate. And herein lies the problem. Creating these experiences is not something you do in addition to your life—it is how to live your life, by creating prosperity, happiness and peace in all you do. That's leadership.

If each person connected what they are already doing in the world to their aspirations of what they wish to see "out there," the world would be a different place in one day. That is the beauty of leadership. You already are impacting the world; you are simply unconscious to the impact you are having. As you consciously connect your everyday activities to the greater whole, your impact expands, as does your own experience of what you desire for others, for you cannot give something to others and not receive it multi-fold yourself.

Remembering Forward—How it Works in the World: Today, recall a time when what you wanted you gave to another. Focus on a time when you found your calling, your purpose, and your connection through selflessly giving the best of you. As you move throughout your day, connect to the memory of service and bring it forward to anchor your purpose and create your

105

future, a future that is created by cultivating for others, what you most desire.

Genuine politics -- every politics worthy of the name -- the only politics I am willing to devote myself to -- is simply a matter of serving those around us: serving the community and serving those who will come after us. Its deepest roots are moral because it is a responsibility expressed through action, to and for the whole—
Vaclav Havel

Mantra: *Every action I take is one of service to world.*

Practice What if There is Nothing Wrong with You: Often the reason people don't choose to help, assist, or guide others is because they feel that if they themselves are not perfect, how they can possibly help others. As you go throughout your day, give to others what you wish to see in the world. If you want more peace, then be peaceful and spread it throughout your day. If you want more environmental sensitivity, then express that in your activities. Connect into the power you have to change now and see how that impacts the people around you.

From My Experience: Being of service and endeavoring to make the world a better place is at the core of my life and work. As a child, I dreamed about how we could improve public housing, make education vibrant and shift health care from its focus on treating illness to cultivating wellness. I am the first to acknowledge my ambitions were a bit out the box and outside the normal focus of a child—and it is true, I knew in my heart these things could be improved for the benefit of the whole.

As my career progressed, I understood that supporting leadership development was the key to allowing these goals to be reached—that we need aligned clear, inspired individuals to address these issues in order for them to be solved. This knowing put me firmly on the outside of the societal and organizational norms that favor the status quo and while professionally there have been many ups and downs, I couldn't abandon these beliefs because it wasn't just about a job or income—it is who I am.

By remaining true to my service to others, my work continues and is an ever- evolving process. By focusing on providing leadership guidance, the opportunities to do so are always showing up. Give who you are and what you can and those who want the same thing will meet you.

3rd Sunday: How Do I Integrate Silence, Nature and Non-Judgment into My Life?

Silence is a source of Great Strength—**Lao Tzu**

How Do I Trust That in Pausing, I Strengthen My Actions?

The fuel of modern life is activity—constant, perpetual motion is the measure of your worth. In your constant desire to prove your worth, you have lost a most essential practice that keeps you connected to your own source of strength: quiet reflection in nature. Here you find the code for the clarity and presence that is needed to navigate successfully in your life so that you are leading it, not the other way around.

You are told silence is golden, and yet contemporary life is filled with everything that keeps it from you—unrelenting electronic devices, traffic and other people. Being immersed in noise has become such a norm that other than being asleep, most people cannot remember the last time they spent even five minutes in silence. And by silence, I mean with no other distractions, not reading or some other activity. Silence as in stillness, presence, peace; and while meditation has gained popularity and is beneficial, it is not a replacement for present, mindful silence that allows you to become alert to your essential nature.

In moments of silence, you can cultivate a connection to the deeper, ever-present "you" that exists beyond titles and roles. As you connect to your true nature, life takes on a richer texture that cannot be experienced while in a frenzy. You see how many of the challenges in your life are created by your lack of mindfulness and the choices of racing thoughts rather than the clarity of choice that comes from calmness and knowing. The wisdom of silence is that you choose how you experience every minute of your life.

Finally, there is nature. Why be silent in nature as opposed to your home, a place of worship or your office at the end of the day. While cultivating silence anywhere is good, in nature it takes on an entirely different feel. You are a natural being, you are connected to the rhythms of life, and unlike plants and other animals, and you struggle through life because of your thoughts. A squirrel is not worried about a mortgage; he trusts that he will create a safe home that will be there for him, and if something happens to it, he creates a new one. A flower isn't concerned about when and how to bloom, it just does. The flow of nature informs you and reminds you that you too are natural, and in the silence of that moment, you glimpse what you already know to be true—that all is well, if you allow it to be.

Remembering Forward—How It Works in the World: Was there a moment in your life when silence rained on you and you knew the answer to the question you've been asking? The stillness of an early morning sunrise? A moment of clarity understood during a walk on the beach? Or perhaps it was bliss that descended during a hike through the woods? Whatever that moment was, most likely in a place outside your typical day, recreate it. Go outside and witness the sunrise even if you aren't on vacation. Find a body of water to sit next to or a forest to walk in. Nearly everyone has the ability to find nature in his or her current life and create that moment of silence. Remember forward, live it and practice it every day.

True silence is the rest of the mind; it is to the spirit what sleep is to the body, nourishment and refreshment—**William Penn**

Mantra: *In silence, I know.*

Practice What if There is Nothing Wrong with You: In silence, in nature, you come face-to-face with the truth, there is nothing wrong with you. There is nothing wrong with the bird whose markings are a bit different from those of the others. There is nothing wrong with the squirrel who needs a midday break from his work. There is nothing wrong with the plant that has not yet bloomed. Everything in nature is perfect as it is—and so are you. From this day forward, use silence and nature as your touchstone for this important truth. From this day on, you are as natural as all these creatures and equally as beautiful.

From My Experience: The practice of silence and connection to nature is at the heart of my ability to be balanced. When life throws a curveball, it is in nature and silence that I find my center and am able to reflect on the various lessons discussed in this book. I chose to live in a naturally beautiful place because I know that the outdoors provides me opportunity to connect fully to myself. It is in this place of connection that I anchor into my leadership and can gracefully move through whatever experience comes.

Being in silence, particularly in nature is powerful because nature allows us to be in harmony with the natural rhythms of life. Plants, animals, insects don't struggle in their existence—the laws of nature guide them and they gently ride the waves. Even in adverse situations, they flow with what is and are more adaptive than humans who allow the mind to make up stories about what is actually happening. When we are silent in nature, we allow this wisdom to suffuse our being. We breathe differently, we find the pause between the thoughts that tells us that we should be different; we let go and can simply be.

By experiencing this blissful state, we can then return to the "reality" of our lives with a fresh perspective, center, calm and clear. This clarity brings peace to your interactions. Your leadership blooms when you are centered and certain in your being—bring opportunities to do this into your life and you will be richly rewarded.

4th Monday: Using my Leadership Skills

If your actions inspire others to dream more, learn more, do more and become more, you are a leader—**John Quincy Adams**

How Do I Lead?

Most people do not see themselves as leaders. The truth is we are all leading in our lives; most of us simply don't understand that we are doing it. The result of not owning your leadership is that outside factors—such as your boss, partner or society—rule your life, so that you take less and less responsibility for choices you could and should be making. Rather than taking control and being aware of the impact we are having in the world, we choose not to think about it, for better or worse. Each person's actions affect people every day; the question from the quote above is, "are your actions inspiring others or not?"

Because you are leading in your life and therefore are a leader, understanding the three fundamentals of leadership are key to success. They are:

- **Communication:** Leadership is relational, which means every interaction you have is based on communication. Leadership is being conscious and aware of all communications, including the messages you send, verbally and non-verbally, to others; and, in turn, what others are saying (and what they truly mean); with a perspective on the biases and filters each party brings that might impact the intent of messages being sent and received. Leaders are constantly bringing clarity, light and truth to all conversations in which they are involved.

- **Conscious Choice:** In each action you take, you make a choice. Do you take the highway or the back roads? Do you wear the navy or the grey suit? Should you vacation at the beach or in the mountains? These questions mostly go undetected as leadership choices, and becoming aware of the hundreds of times each day you affirm your leadership is critical to understanding the choices when the stakes are higher. Do you speak up about what isn't working within your organization? Do you choose to engage in a way that addresses issues or creates more problems? Are you giving your best? Are you in the right position for your talents? These choices are made each day as well, except that too many choose to believe that the answers come from outside of their control. Leaders cultivate conscious choice by understanding that every action is within their control—and in doing so; each one is approached in the best possible way.

- **Conflict Resolution:** Inherent in interactions between people is conflict—it is inevitable. Yet, most people are loath to acknowledge it, let alone engage in it. Leaders understand conflict as a natural part of life, and they don't allow varying perspectives or disagreements to knock them off-center. Leaders, through effective communication and choice, understand that conflict is a tool for growth and use the opportunity to fortify their own values and clarity and to open the dialogue for others to do the same. When a leader shows up open, clear and confident, it is difficult for conflict to flourish.

Therefore, whether you view yourself as a leader or not, you are. The choice you have is to take hold of this understanding and be your best or to pretend you exist outside this truth. The result is either a life driven by you or by outside circumstances. The former is a much more fun, easy and healthy way to live.

Remembering Forward—How It Works in the World: When asked to remember a time when they felt powerful, people often recall moments in which they were being of service to others. It could have been the success of an event they organized, an election won, or the achievement of a group with whom they were working. Whatever the experience, the seed of power came from helping others to flourish. It is a wonder that "leaders" are viewed as the ones who accumulate power for their own ends rather than serving the needs of the whole. In remembering forward today, let go of the outdated and ineffective definition of authoritative leadership, and connect into those moments of true power—the times when you served others through your strengths and all of you were better for it. Take that feeling into today and lead through your service to others. After all, leadership is love in action.

Power isn't control at all—power is strength, and giving that strength to others. A leader isn't someone who forces others to make him stronger; a leader is someone willing to give his strength to others that they may have the strength to stand on their own— **Beth Revis**

Mantra: *I am a leader.*

Practice What if There is Nothing Wrong with You: Effective communication, conscious choice and conflict resolution are predicated on your showing up in each moment with clarity about yourself and your desired contribution. These core leadership principles often become difficult not because the actions themselves are challenging; rather, because you are unclear, closed or feel there is something wrong with you. If you believe there is something wrong with you, then it becomes impossible to be open and clear when you are hiding from your leadership. Using each of the three core leadership elements today—communication, conscious choice and conflict resolution—engage as a leader with each person with whom you interact; a leader with whom there is nothing wrong.

From My Experience: Leadership has been the focus of my work throughout my career. It became my passion, my desired contribution when I understood that leaders could, do and need to exist everywhere in society. You can't lead without first becoming a leader and my life is how I test my model, learn and grow then guide others from a place of experience.

It isn't always easy to lead life this way, of feeling like there are unrealistic standards or the judgments of others clouding my path. What I've realized is that leading my life as the best I can be is the way I find happiness, fulfillment and impact—that the moment I step away from my leadership things start to go awry. As it is with all of us, we know the gifts we have to share with others and how we offer them defines our leadership. When we are not aligned to offer our gifts in the best way, life will continue to show us the way back to our path. So leading, staying true to ourselves and being our best are really all one in the same and the key to happiness and satisfaction—making the choice to lead a natural one.

4th Tuesday: Communicating Who I Am

The authentic self is the soul made visible—**Sarah Ban Breathnach**

Do I Communicate Who I Am to Others?

The question, "Who Am I?" is important for you to answer. Equally important is communicating clearly and consistently, *who you are* to others. Understanding who you are grounds you in the world. Without a clear understanding of you, your talents, strengths, passion and desired contribution, it is challenging to align your communication and actions. Authentic leaders know who they are and are able to communicate it to others in every communication. Many people are focused on image or brand—that is, being consistent in how they look and present themselves so that others immediately know them. Yet, how one looks, is only the beginning of understanding that they are. By delving deeper into your being as the origin of your communications—that is, the self that creates your consistent words, actions and deeds—means that your image or brand is more than skin deep: it is you.

Revealing your true self to others is intimidating because you harbor fears, anger, grief and other feelings you may wish to hide. The challenge you face with this behavior, though, is that in hiding parts of yourself, you dampen your own light *and* the process of hiding creates unease in others. Others don't know that what you are hiding is based on your own concerns about yourself; instead, it comes across as not trusting the other person. Being open and clear about who you are with others creates the way for you to expand your true nature and allows others to do the same.

Remembering Forward—How It Works in the World: Some of the most cherished moments in your intimate relationships are the times when you feel unconditionally loved for who you are. Naked physically, emotionally and spiritually, you allow yourself to be seen, held and loved for who you are. Reflect on those moments today, whether they are with a family member, friend or lover, and then bring the essence of being disarmed and disarming to your interactions today. You will be surprised by how much love for *you* reveals itself in your life.

Today you are you, that is truer than true. There is nobody else who is your-er than you. – **Dr. Seuss**

Mantra: *I am completely open with others about Who I Am.*

Practice What if There is Nothing Wrong with You: Ask somebody to stand naked before a group and speak, and chances are, he or she would laugh—for a variety of reasons. Now think of public speaking while fully clothed with your soul naked. Could you stand before others and allow them to see you? The reason you don't want to do it, physically, emotionally, mentally, spiritually, is that you don't want people to see your flaws. If you were a swimsuit model, being naked in front of others wouldn't be such a big deal, as you would have a beautiful body by society's standards. And in the same way, each person is beautiful on the inside and out, so shows that person to all those with whom you meet today—as there is nothing wrong with you!

From My Experience: Early in my career I was all too aware of the things that were "wrong" with me: I didn't have enough experience to be doing the job, I didn't feel good about my body, I wasn't sure others liked and supported me. The list was long. As I assumed more positions of authority and had to speak in front of others, I prepared thoroughly for every speaking engagement or big meeting—if I was going to be presenting my flawed self; I was going to do everything in my power to make it appear flawless.

In addition to the time, it took to (over) prepare and the stress it caused, two things became clear. The first was that despite my diligent preparation, things still went "wrong:" my hair clip broke at the last minute; I couldn't find a set of notes, or someone else showed up to the meeting wanting something different from me. These small occurrences created much heartache because I thought my value was in the performance and not in me.

The other stumbling block was that in my rigid preparation, I lost my ability to be spontaneous and free because I was afraid that if people saw me they would only see the flaws. Herein lies one of the gifts of living the leadership choice, when you identify your talents and strengths you own them for yourself first. When you know your gifts, it is easier to let people see the real you because the focus is where it belongs, on what you uniquely bring to the table and not the minor "imperfections" you obsess about to yourself.

As I understood this phenomenon, I realized that people want to connect with my passion, to hear my insights and engage in conversation with me. They didn't care if my hair was up or down, if every word I said was elegant prose or if I didn't have all the answers in that moment—what they wanted was for me to show-up, as my best and do my best.

When I let go of the hiding and allowed the real me to emerge magic happened. People liked what I was doing, they were more engaged and wanted more of what I was offering—and I had a lot more fun. I was enjoyable and they enjoyed me because they too are real people and the more I led that way, it inspired them to be the same.

4th Wednesday: Being Clear About What I Want

God has allowed some magical reversal to occur,
So that you see the scorpion pit
as an object of desire,
and all the beautiful expanse around it,
as dangerous and swarming with snakes—**Mevlana Rumi** (1207 - 1273)

Am I Clear About What I Want To Create In My Life?

When you are unclear about what you truly want in your life, you feel disempowered because the outcomes you are achieving in your life aren't what you desire. Lack of clarity has serious consequences, because you get what you want. It is your lack of focus on the essence of desire that causes what you are saying and what you are doing to be misaligned. You become upset when what you say you want on the surface isn't showing up in your life, when the reality is what you might be asking for doesn't align with your deepest wants, or it is being hijacked by the belief that you can't have or don't deserve it. Yesterday, you cleared the way for you to know yourself without pretense and to share it with others; today, explore the true essence of your desires. What is it you wish to have in your life? Deeper, loving relationships? Greater abundance? More peace? Moments of true joy?

Bypassing the surface of your desire to get at its core is essential because most people get lost and/or sidetracked by what "it looks like" rather becoming totally clear about what it is. If you want greater abundance in your life, does it matter if you win the lottery or get a raise? In both cases, you get what you desire, and it might be even better than you imagined. Where people get lost is in thinking, "I will never get a raise in this job," so wanting a new job becomes the focus rather than the desire you truly wanted, which was more abundance. In the manifestation of what you think you desire, i.e., a new job, you likely don't get what you wanted, which was a raise; you just created another job that doesn't pay you what you want as well.

Remembering Forward—How It Works in the World: Your imagination *is* a preview of the realization of what you want to create in your life, and your past can govern your future if you allow it; however, the choice between the two lives in the now. Today in remembering forward, be aware of how often-past negative experiences color your actions rather than open accepting thoughts on how to move forward toward what you truly desire. Reflect on what is in your life now. Can you trace to see that what you now have is what you once wished for—and now that it is here, was it truly, what you wanted? If not, remember forward to the times when you were clearly connected to your authentic desires and how it made you feel to realize those. Starting today, consciously create what it is you want in your life and the world by remembering just how powerful you are.

Our imagination is the preview to life's coming attractions – **Albert Einstein**

Mantra: *I am clear and connected to my authentic desires.*

Practice What if There is Nothing Wrong with You: By this point, you understand it is your own belief in barriers and wounds that keeps you from living as you desire. From a starting point of there is nothing wrong with you their lifeblood ceases to exist. Today, find time to reflect on your deepest desires—not what they look like; rather, focus on how you wish to feel when experiencing them. At their core, these experiences will likely cause you to feel more alive, joyful and loving. In practicing what if there is nothing wrong with you today, allow yourself to be more alive, joyful and loving—and observe the difference. What you desire will come in wonderful, surprising ways.

From My Experience: There are times when being a leader seems difficult. Being authentic takes courage; being aligned requires mindfulness and achieving results needs energy. At some point, everyone feels the weight of it all and longs for an escape from walking their leadership in the world. It is at those times that we are reminded of what it is we want to create in our lives. Ultimately, we want joy, contentment and peace.

With as much passion as I have for the subject, I too experience these times when I need to pause and focus on what it is I truly desire. When the doing to achieve becomes paramount it is exhausting and it is my indicator that I am focusing on the externalities and not on my experience of it. This is when the clarity about what I want to create is realized, I can re-focus on what ultimately matters to me, and that is to feel good.

When I own the power to create the narrative, I feel better. Are things a disaster or have I simply hit a bump in the road? My leadership in choosing my thoughts allows me to create the feeling I desire and when I line-up my beliefs and emotions first, the actions and results are better. The choice to lead always results in progress and growth and sometimes all we need to do is focus on ourselves when we lose our way in serving others.

4th Thursday: Using Your Passion as Power

Every great dream begins with a dreamer. Always remember, you have within you the strength, the patience, and the passion to reach for the stars to change the world—**Harriet Tubman**

Is My Passion Fueling My Actions?

Each day you awaken with a full tank of the greatest asset in our lives—your time and attention. One hundred sixty-eight hours of consciousness a week, 112 hours awake in seven 16-hour days; how are you using your gift of time? Are you bleary from numbing yourself with various substances? Are you slow because you are sad about some condition in your life? Or are you alive to your experiences and engaging with the world as a leader in your life?

If you are like most people, you fall somewhere in between the extremes. You want aliveness, and the way you get it is through aligning with your passion and living it each day. Passion is an intense desire for something—and that something is what makes you. We've discussed identifying the contribution you wish to make to the world; now is the time to ask yourself if you are pursuing it each day or not. When you allow yourself to follow your passions, things change around you because you are changed. When you are open and inspired, you are magnetically drawn to conditions and circumstances that bring you joy and allow you to share your gifts with others.

When your day is fueled with passion, flow happens. When you feel stuck or reluctant, look for the root of the issue, as it lies with your inability to believe you can pursue your passion. Then do something, anything, to show yourself and the world otherwise, and before you know it, living your passion will be the only fuel in your life.

Remembering Forward—How It Works in the World: As you remember forward today, reflect on a time when you felt truly inspired, when you wanted to pursue something simply because it felt so good, and you knew it was the best possible thing for you to be doing. Allow that feeling of expansiveness, knowing and confidence to permeate your actions today. Your default mode is to believe that you can't be the best of yourself. Today, remember forward by bringing the knowing that you can be passionate about all you do, and in doing so, you create the fuel for your future—a future that is based on being your best and leading in your life.

Passion is one great force that unleashes creativity, because if you're passionate about something, then you're more willing to take risks—**Yo Yo Ma**

Mantra: *My actions are fueled by my passion.*

Practice What if There is Nothing Wrong with You: Passionately fueled actions at their essence are self-love, as the most loving thing you can do is actively to live that love for yourself. Leadership is love in action. True leaders are those who know and love themselves so that they can effortlessly put their gifts into the world in service to others. There is nothing wrong with you or your passion. The thing that most often is lacking is the courage to take action. The time has come to be your best, to lead and live your passion—every day. In some way today, have the courage to live your passion with complete abandon and be the person you truly are and share it with at least one other person, giving the gift of your passion to another.

From My Experience

When I fully allow myself to live into my passion for leadership, something amazing happens—I effortlessly cross paths with people who want insights about their leadership. These synchronistic meetings may be with friends, acquaintances or strangers. They may be individuals who will become clients or those that simply needed a kind word or keen insight to help them along. Whatever it is, I am grateful for these times because it is a confirmation that others need my passion.

Herein is the great power behind living your passion, it not only serves others it serves you because you get to live what you love and see its positive impact on the world. Living a win-win life of passion starts with you and your decision to be and do what you love. When you have the courage to take your passion into the world you stoke the flame in others. That's leadership, being your best and inspiring it in others.

4th Friday: Creating Community

Community is a sign that love is possible in a materialistic world where people so often either ignore or fight each other. It is a sign that we don't need a lot of money to be happy—in fact, the opposite—**Jean Vanier, *Community And Growth***

Do I Have A Community that Supports Me? Do I Support My Community?

Leadership has often been thought of as a solitary pursuit, that it is the person on top, alone and controlling. This twisted version of leadership has created innumerable problems in our world. Leadership is love in action; it is action based on the understanding that what you do for and to yourself, you do to all others. Our interconnectedness remains one of the fundamental stumbling blocks for the great individualistic culture in the United States. You are not an island; what you do affects others. As a society, we can honor individual expression and, at the same time, the connection of each individual to the entire community.

A supportive community is a reflection of how much you support others. Is community important to you? If it is not a priority, you can expand your leadership by engaging with and for others. Service to others is where you live your purpose. By building community, you not only serve, you bring others to the table and offer them the opportunity to serve and give their passion to the world as well. Where you feel called to give is where there is a need. Your engagement sparks a network of people who are available and ready to give with you, thereby creating a beautiful web of giving and receiving—love in action. Leaders start the process, they keep it going and they bring others to the table to join in because leaders understand that nothing happens in isolation, and no person can do it alone. As others come to the table, they too become leaders, for themselves and the others in their world.

Remembering Forward—How It Works in the World: Do you remember a time in your life when you needed something and someone appeared who was able to give it to you? Perhaps it was advice with a challenge, or maybe it was a skill they had that you needed to move forward on a project. Whatever it was, their gift allowed you to move forward. This is what we do for each other every day all the time; we just don't acknowledge and consciously cultivate it. Today, remember forward, recalling when someone offered you what you needed at the moment you needed it—and today do the same for another person. Make a note to check back in on that person in one week; the bond that is created will surprise you through your actions, a bond that starts a community.

*No man is an island, entire of itself; every man is a piece of the continent, a part of the main. If a clod be washed away by the sea, Europe is the less . . . any man's death diminishes me, because I am involved in mankind, and therefore never send to know for whom the bells tolls; it tolls for thee—***John Donne, *No Man Is An Island - Meditation XVII***

Mantra: *My actions build community.*

Practice what if there is nothing wrong with you: Too often, you don't offer yourself in service to your community because you believe that you are not perfect or perfected in your gifts. By denying these gifts to the community and to those in it, you are denying yourself. Believe in who you are and what you bring, and move forward today to consciously create community. Build bridges that bring various talents to the table by acknowledging the gifts in others and see how they reflect back to your own.

From My Experience: One of the most common and saddest occurrences with my clients is feeling that they don't have a community that would support their passion and leadership. They believe that if the people around them knew who they truly were it would change the nature of their relationship. I've had gifted musicians who didn't want co-workers to know of their talent because they feared it would make them seem less serious about their current policy work. It is true for many people who hide their passion away as they pursue careers that leave little room for the creative joys. The tragedy is not only for the individual who ignores their passion; it also keeps communities from authentically forming around what really matters. Who else has complimentary passions that could ignite connections, lost in the pursuit of looking professional in front of your peers?

Creativity, aliveness, engagement are what make our communities vital and sharing our gifts is how we nurture those elements in the circles in which we live and work. Bringing our gifts forward is the glue—because it is the sharing that makes it real. A musical policy expert brings value to the workplace because there is a harmonious way she is oriented in her leadership and when she allows others to see her passion she offers new ways of connecting to her and understanding her leadership. In seeing the whole person, her leadership makes sense and who knows; a rival may have a great voice that they learn synergize together at work and in music.

Everyone longs to be a part of something greater and creating the greater whole can only happen when everyone comes bearing gifts—their gifts. I've seen it happen time and again, that when people share themselves with other they find these connections, the passion grows and workplaces become communities—communities led by passionate people.

4th Saturday: Taking Action

There are risks and costs to action. But they are far less than the long-range risks of comfortable inaction—**John F. Kennedy**

Am I Taking Action In Alignment with My Leadership?

As you near the end of the 28-day process, you arrive where you started at leadership—love in action. Even if you understand yourself, know what you want to contribute and align your life with that knowledge, you aren't effective until you act on it. It is through action that your true self becomes real. Many people are "busy," yet they are not taking action rooted in their leadership to create the results they wish to see in the world. When we were an agrarian and then an industrialized country, it was easy to see the fruits of our labors; the evidence was in the plowed field or the number of cars coming off an assembly line. In the information age, we have replaced focused activity that leads to results in favor of frenzied activity that often draws down on our creativity rather than adding to it. We use quantity rather than quality as the measure of effectiveness—yes, we organize our lives to spend inordinate amounts of time in an office, but what are we really accomplishing?

Various studies document that we only spend a few hours a day, or less, being productive because unimportant issues caused by a lack of leadership on everyone's part take precedent. As you begin to take charge of your life, act in alignment with your leadership and what you wish to create in the world, your actions follow suit. Your interest in office gossip or mindlessly perusing the Internet is less enticing as you are enlivened by true contribution and progress toward your goals. If what you are doing is not a true reflection of the leader you are, stop doing it. If you find yourself doing something that doesn't inspire you, ask yourself why you are wasting your most precious resource.

Remembering Forward—How It Works in the World: Reflect on a time when you absolutely LOVED what you were doing. Can you remember that feeling of timelessness? Bring forward those emotions of joy, excitement, and aliveness. Whatever you are remembering, it was likely something that you are good at, something that you always wanted to do and something that benefitted others as well as yourself. These feelings and moments are in short supply in your life because you've decided you can't live this way—except that you can. Today, bring those feelings into your day. Bring the dream forward into this moment and take one action that makes it more real in your life. If you do just one thing every day to achieve your goals, you will realize them faster than you can imagine.

Love begins at home, and it is not how much we do... but how much love we put in that action—**Mother Teresa**

Mantra: *My actions express my priorities.*

Practice What if There is Nothing Wrong with You: One of the greatest excuses for inaction is the fallback that something is wrong with you that keeps you from taking action on my goals. The trick is that as long as you allow yourself this excuse, then it will never be time to take action. Every moment is the perfect moment to do what is right for you in service to others and in creation of the life you want to lead. Today, practice not only that there is nothing wrong with you; also expand the belief that there is nothing wrong with the now. Now is the only time you can take action, so let go of believing that it isn't time to live your dreams, and know that it is the only time you can.

From My Experience: Inspired action is a concept that energizes me because it is one of the most tangible. Our days are filled with doing things and when I can connect my activities with what I am truly passionate about my mood shifts. I simply ask myself, "Why am I doing this?"

In asking this question, I am looking for a part of cleaning up after a meal, paying the bills or going to a volunteer meeting that is connected to my true self. By focusing on my authentic enjoyment of a clean home, financial integrity or contribution to my community I align my actions with my inspiration rather than my frustrations and boredom. Being a leader doesn't mean that you rid yourself of the lower emotions, it means that you consciously choose not to indulge them.

With just a moment or two of consideration before taking action to ensure that you are aligned and connected with your true self—shifts will occur for you and those around you.

4th Sunday: The Upward Spiral

We are at our very best, and we are happiest, when we are fully engaged in work we enjoy on the journey toward the goal we've established for ourselves. It gives meaning to our time off and comfort to our sleep. It makes everything else in life so wonderful, so worthwhile—**Earl Nightingale**

Am I Committed to the Journey?

You came to the leadership development process because you felt the call to something greater. What you found is that in wanting to live more fully the first step is to shift yourself and as you do so, so does everything in your life. While you are experiencing the results of examining your leadership through this process, it is important to continue the work. We are creatures of habit and conditioning, and the moment you lose focus on yourself and your leadership, you fall. For most, it will take the next downturn, crisis or malaise to kick-start the process again. In truth, the process never ends; it is you who chooses to be aware of being in it or not.

For those who wish to stay true to themselves, the awareness of the continuing journey and attention and attending to the leader in you is essential and unending. If you can find the joy in the leadership practice, each step becomes easier. Like eating well and exercising, you may experience ebbs and flows, and the practice always warrants your attention. This book was written with the intention that it becomes a companion, living with you through your life cycles to guide you, continually to awaken you in your journey and to remind you how you can live it at your very best. Use this and other resources to keep your practice alive, and the challenges that come will be fewer, and you will handle them with increasing grace and assuredness.

Remembering Forward—How It Works in the World: In remembering forward today, recall a time when you felt that you had arrived, where you were done, or had reached the pinnacle. Perhaps it was graduation, or winning an athletic event or securing the corner office. Can you remember how good you felt to have finally achieved a long-sought-after goal? Next, allow yourself to reflect on how long it was before the yearning for the next challenge emerged—it wasn't that you were unhappy with your achievement, it is that you are designed to want to stretch for the next peak, always. Longing for the goal is essential and working toward it and enjoying the process is how we live—the achievement of it is fleeting. Remember forward today to a time when you allowed yourself to love the process and the steps in between, and bring that excitement into your life today—and every day, as it is the only way to move forward with happiness.

It is good to have an end to journey toward; but it is the journey that matters, in the end—**Ernest Hemingway**

Mantra: *I commit myself to my leadership development today and every day.*

Practice what if there is nothing wrong with you: You are perfect, this moment is perfect and you have the ability to choose how you lead in it and where you go. If you stay focused in the now and trust in yourself, there is nothing wrong with you and where you are going. Staying present is the greatest gift you can give to yourself and to others. Live with the knowing that you are a leader in your life, and you are choosing *everything* that is in your life. If you don't like something that is showing up— lead. If you love what is happening now—keep leading. And if you want to contribute something more—lead. You are a leader, and there is nothing wrong with you.

From My Experience: Early in adulthood, I longed to have all the various aspects of my life in a good place—work, relationship, family, friends, community. Things were good in some areas and not so good in others and then it would shift as issues came up where it had been peaceful and challenging situations resolved themselves. I felt I couldn't be happy until they were all good, so putting off happiness became the norm.

In engaging with the leadership journey, I came to understand that the process is my life and that it will never be perfect. It is a practice that requires mindfulness and is always providing new insights as to place where I can shift to change what is showing up or not in my life. I rely on books, quotes, insights and guidance to help me along my path and ultimately it is by trusting my leadership that I move forward. Whatever supports you to go deeper, to understand and embrace that which you already know to be true for yourself, keep doing it? It is this practice that will keep you on your path and lead you where you most want to go—to living the leadership choice.

Conclusion

Congratulations on having the courage, clarity and diligence to move through the 28 daily lessons. It does not matter if you completed them in four weeks, in sequence or you accessed them when you felt called to a particular day and topic, what matters is that you answered the call to lead.

By choosing to lead, you have set forth waves of change in your life. By now, you will have experienced the shifts in how you are feeling and likely have seen other results show up in your work and relationships. A few common experiences for people who are engaged with this process include:

- **Euphoria followed by a "real life" wake-up call**: As you begin living the leadership choice, you feel good and see the results of leading in your life. You feel better, you address challenges that have been plaguing you and allow the minor irritants in your life to fade away; and just as you feel all is going your way, "real life" enters to remind you that you are not in control of external events. Life always will be throwing curve balls, the key is to choose if you are going to allow someone's pitch to determine your choice to lead—or not. Choosing to lead does not mean that life is perfect, although as you progress it will become increasingly easier, it does mean, however, that you can do to know that you are leading in each moment. With this knowledge, you can address the challenge gracefully and move through it with ease—well, at least more ease than when you were not leading in your life.

- **Leading become exhausting**: When we shift our focus to the choice we have to lead in our lives, the invitation to lead everywhere all the time becomes intoxicating. As people begin to catch the wave of leadership, they want to do it all the time—at work, in their community, with their families, their partners, etc. and in so doing, can burn themselves out. I encourage people to know that they are leading in their lives at all time *and* to understand the elegance of allowing greater focus in some areas while allowing other areas to rest with softer attention. This doesn't mean don't lead, it means knowing when to expand rapidly and when to allow simple mindful leadership to hold the space of excellence without having to expand it in the moment.

- **My current life doesn't match my leadership**: This is the greatest challenge and occurrence for people choosing to lead. Your choice to engage in the leadership journey does not guarantee that those around you will choose to do the same. As a result of your leadership blossoming, of you choosing to live your talents and strengths, of you making your contribution to the work and aligning your life to these fundamental principles, the people around you begin to look and feel very different. They have to. You created these situations and relationships when you were not leading, so it is no wonder people don't feel the same and your relationships take on a different patina—which can be frightening. The key is to stay on your path and to offer those about whom you care the choice to lead as well. Some will head the call and be grateful you inspired them. Others will not be ready, or not choose to lead at this time in their lives. It is okay. Allowing those who are not prepared to walk with you to choose for themselves, without judgment of you or them, is important. All you can do is choose to lead and inspire that choice in others—it is up to them to make the decision for themselves. If you are open to people making those choices for themselves, you will find you will always be met by like-minded people, you just won't know who they are until you walk through each day as a leader.

My concluding thought for you is to keep moving—to choose to lead every day. Some days it will be easier than others. There are times when allowing yourself to rest in leadership rather than actively pursuing it will occur. No differently than a hike through the woods, there are times to sit and rest, others to stop and admire the view and those moments when survival may mean to keep going despite the fear and adversity. The key is to trust yourself, to believe in your leadership and to know you will always reach your goal—and that by choosing to lead you will find yourself at greater peaks, more and more often.

Lead—the world needs the gifts of your journey and you deserve to live life of leadership.